The Cyrus Cylinder and Ancient Persia

The Cyrus Cylinder and Ancient Persia

A New Beginning for the Middle East

John Curtis

With an introductory essay by Neil MacGregor
and a translation of the Cyrus Cylinder by Irving Finkel

The British Museum

IRAN HERITAGE

This book is published to accompany the touring exhibition 'The Cyrus Cylinder and Ancient Persia' at Arthur M. Sackler Gallery, Smithsonian Institution, Washington D.C., 9 March–28 April 2013; Museum of Fine Arts, Houston, 3 May–14 June 2013; The Metropolitan Museum of Art, New York, 20 June–4 August 2013; Asian Art Museum, San Francisco, 9 August–22 September 2013; and J. Paul Getty Museum at the Getty Villa, Los Angeles, 2 October–2 December 2013

© 2013 The Trustees of the British Museum

John Curtis has asserted the right to be identified as the author of this work.

First published in 2013 by The British Museum Press
A division of The British Museum Company Ltd
38 Russell Square, London WC1B 3QQ
britishmuseum.org/publishing

A catalogue record of this book is available from the British Library

ISBN 978-0-7141-1187-2

Designed by Bobby Birchall
Printed in Hong Kong

The papers used in this book are recyclable products and the manufacturing processes conform to the environmental regulations of the country of origin.

Frontispiece: The Cyrus Cylinder, 539–538 BC, excavated in Babylon in 1879. Baked clay, length 22.86 cm, diameter 10.0 cm. British Museum, BM 90920 (1880,0617.1941)

The majority of the objects illustrated in this book are from the collection of the British Museum. Further information about the Museum and its collection can be found at britishmuseum.org.

Contents

Sponsor's Acknowledgements

IHF
AMERICA

IHF America proudly recognizes the generous sponsorship and support of the following organizations and individuals, without whose support this tour would not be possible.

WASHINGTON D.C.

Dalia & Hossein Fateh
Alireza Ittihadieh
Hassan and Nezhat Khosrowshahi
Mehrdad Moayedi
Angelina & Alex Vahabzadeh
Soudavar Memorial Foundation

HOUSTON

Morteza Bahrloo
Mr. & Mrs. Alan B. Chaveleh
Farideh & Jafar Davoody
Suzanne & Ali Ebrahimi
Shoaleh and Asghar Nosrati
Sherry and Ardeshir Tajvari

NEW YORK CITY

Ansary Foundation

Akbar A. Lari
Iranian American Jewish Federation of New York
Nowruz Commission

SAN FRANCISCO

Tina & Hamid Moghadam
Bita Daryabari & Dr. Reza Malek

in collaboration with
Public Affairs Alliance of Iranian Americans

LOS ANGELES

FARHANG FOUNDATION

Iran Heritage Foundation Foreword

It is a great pleasure for the Iran Heritage Foundation to partner the British Museum and the Smithsonian Institution in bringing the traveling exhibition 'The Cyrus Cylinder and Ancient Persia' to the United States. The Cyrus Cylinder is an iconic object for many Iranians and it is closely associated with the foundation of the Ancient Persian Empire by Cyrus the Great. As it is the remit of the IHF to promote and preserve the cultural heritage of Iran, it is particularly appropriate that IHF America should sponsor this tour and provide the opportunity for many to see this unique object. The other objects included in the exhibition highlight the contributions made by Ancient Persia to the development of civilization, and range from exquisite jewellery and gold tableware from the Oxus Treasure to examples of Old Persian cuneiform. Also included are probably the earliest representation of an Iranian priest and the famous cylinder seal of Darius the Great.

We are proud that our institutional partnership with the British Museum is now of long standing. We have supported an annual IHF Fellow at the British Museum since 1998. We sponsored the very successful special exhibition 'Forgotten Empire: the World of Ancient Persia' in 2005–6 as well as the accompanying international conference and the proceedings, which have now been published through an IHF publications grant. In 2007 a member of our board of trustees sponsored the new Rahim Irvani Gallery of Ancient Iran which has now become the permanent home of the Cyrus Cylinder at the British Museum. 'Forgotten Empire' was followed by the equally attractive exhibition 'Shah 'Abbas: the Remaking of Iran', again sponsored by IHF. We have similarly entered into an institutional partnership relationship with the Smithsonian Institution's Freer and Sackler Galleries where an IHF grant has secured the establishment of its first Iranian arts curator.

We discussed the idea of this tour first in 2007 with Neil McGregor, the Director of the British Museum. Neil has been a source of vision, energy and inspiration throughout the history of our association with the British Museum. Dr John Curtis and Clare Eardley, our counterparts for the tour at the British Museum, have worked diligently and enthusiastically to curate and manage the multitude of institutional coordination and logistics issues which a complex tour of this nature entails. We are grateful to Dr Julian Raby for embracing the importance of the tour from the outset and encouraging us all to set our sights high.

This tour would not have been possible without the enthusiastic support of the Iranian American community at large who, with their large and small donations, joined us in IHF America to make this a reality. We thus dedicate this touring exhibition to them. Our special thanks goes to some of the prominent members of our community: Hamid Moghadam for his vision and leadership in underwriting the San Francisco visit and to Ali Razi and his fellow trustees at the Farhang Foundation for making the largest single contribution in covering the costs of the Los Angeles visit, to name just a few.

Vahid Alaghband
Chairman
Iran Heritage Foundation

Alireza Rastegar
Chairman
IHF America

Director's Foreword

In 2005–6 we organized a pioneering exhibition at the British Museum about ancient Iran entitled 'Forgotten Empire: the World of Ancient Persia' that was seen by over 150,000 people. The aim of this exhibition was to show the splendid civilization of ancient Persia and how much it had contributed to the world. Ancient Persia has often been unfavourably contrasted in the West with ancient Greece, Persian despotism versus Greek democracy, but as the exhibition sought to demonstrate this is a simplistic notion that is far from the truth. One of the highlights of this exhibition was the Cyrus Cylinder, an object charged with more meaning than practically any other in the British Museum. Rightly, the Cylinder has come to acquire iconic status around the world.

What makes the Cyrus Cylinder such a special object? It is a barrel-shaped clay cylinder inscribed in Babylonian cuneiform that was buried in the foundations of Babylon after Cyrus captured the city in 539 BC. It describes how Cyrus entered Babylon at the invitation of the Babylonian god Marduk, and then proceeded to send back to the shrines from which they had been seized by his Babylonian predecessors statues of various gods, together with the people who lived in the shrines. These enlightened acts, which have been interpreted as allowing freedom of worship and repatriating deported peoples, have earned Cyrus a reputation as a liberal and enlightened monarch, just as he is portrayed in the biblical tradition.

In 2010 the Trustees of the British Museum lent the Cyrus Cylinder to Iran, and it was exhibited in the National Museum in Tehran where it was seen by up to half a million visitors.

The popularity of this exhibition in Tehran was very gratifying, as it is a central aim of the Trustees of the British Museum to make important and iconic objects accessible to as many people as possible, by sending them to special exhibitions around the world. At the time of the Tehran exhibition interest was expressed in sending the Cylinder to the USA, where it might be seen by American Iranians, Jews and Zoroastrians, for whom it has special significance and, we hope, many others. It is particularly appropriate for the Cylinder to be coming to the USA because Cyrus himself was a guiding light for the Founding Fathers. Thanks to Xenophon's *Cyropaedia*, he was thought to embody the qualities of the perfect king, and *Cyropaedia* and *The Prince* by Machiavelli were required reading for aspiring statesmen. Thomas Jefferson is even said to have owned two copies of *Cyropaedia*.

I am delighted that the generosity of the Iran Heritage Foundation has made the tour possible. We also thank the Arthur M. Sackler Gallery, Smithsonian Institution for their partnership as well as the Museum of Fine Arts, Houston, the Metropolitan Museum of Art, the Asian Art Museum, San Francisco and the J. Paul Getty Museum at the Getty Villa who are also hosting the exhibition.

Neil MacGregor
Director
British Museum

The Many Meanings of the Cyrus Cylinder

Neil MacGregor

The things we make have one defining characteristic: they usually last longer than we do. We perish, they endure. We have one life, they have many lives, and in each of those lives – at different times, and at different places – they may mean many different things.

This exhibition traces through two and a half thousand years the biography of one particular object – an inscription buried at the foundation of a building in ancient Babylon shortly after 539 BC.

It is an unprepossessing thing, about the size of a rugby football. It was made of wet clay, fashioned into the shape of a cylinder with tapering ends, densely covered with very small writing, and then fired in a kiln. It has been knocked about over the centuries, and several bits of it are now missing.

Yet today this object is not just a major document of world history. It is also, I believe, a significant player in the politics of the Near East, a central part of the story of both Iran and Israel. Its different meanings offer the world many ways of thinking about the past and, more important, the future of the region. It is an object of many stories, not all yet at an end, and many of which have great resonance in the United States.

The tale begins in the Iran–Iraq war, in that series of events which culminated in the invasion of Iraq by foreign forces, the removal of a despotic ruler and instant and welcome regime change. I want to start with one moment in that sequence of events which will be familiar to many – Belshazzar's feast. The Iran–Iraq war of 539 BC – the struggle between the Babylonian and the Persian empires – was one of the great turning points in world history. Its most famous episode is the subject of Rembrandt's painting, now in the National Gallery in London, illustrating a text from the prophet Daniel in the Hebrew scriptures. You all roughly know the legend.

Belshazzar, regent of Babylon, was a successor of King Nebuchadnezzar, who had conquered Israel, sacked Jerusalem, and taken a large number of the Jews back to Babylon. And not only the Jews. He had also ransacked and

Rembrandt Harmenszoon van Rijn,
Belshazzar's Feast, c. 1636–8.
oil on canvas, 167.6 x 209.2 cm.
National Gallery, London (NG6350)

desecrated the Temple. And the great ceremonial gold vessels of the Temple in Jerusalem had been removed to Babylon. Belshazzar, Daniel tells us, decided to hold a feast. And in order to make the feast more memorable, he added the spice of sacrilege to the rest of the entertainment, and brought out the Jerusalem temple vessels.

Belshazzar was already at war with the neighbouring Iranians, with the king of Persia. And that night, Daniel tells us, at the height of the festivities a mysterious hand appeared and wrote on the wall, 'You are weighed in the balance and found wanting, and your kingdom is handed over to the Medes and the Persians.' Rembrandt shows us those fateful words, written in Hebrew script, and Belshazzar and his guests looking at them in terror-struck incomprehension. That very night, just as the writing predicted, Cyrus, king of the Persians, entered Babylon and the whole regime of Belshazzar fell. It is, of course, a great moment in the history of the Jewish people. It's also a great yarn, and one we all know: 'The writing on the wall' has become part of our everyday language.

What happened next was hardly less remarkable, and is where our Cylinder enters the story. Cyrus, king of the Persians, entered Babylon without a fight and the great empire of Babylon, which ran from central southern Iraq to the Mediterranean, fell into his hands. Soon afterwards Cyrus made a declaration to his new subjects. And that is what this Cylinder records: how the ruler, guided by God, had toppled the despot and was going to bring freedom to the people. In ringing Babylonian phrases – it was written in Babylonian – he says, 'I am Cyrus, king of all the universe, the great king, the powerful king, king of Babylon, king of the four quarters of the world'. As you can see, the Babylonian scribes were not shy of hyperbole. But the text on the Cylinder is in effect the press release of a victorious military commander, eager to win over the conquered population, insisting on his limitless power and on a divine sanction for his invasion.

And what is the great king, the powerful king, the king of the four quarters of the world going to do? He goes on to say that, having conquered Babylon, he will at once let the peoples whom the Babylonian kings – Nebuchadnezzar and Nabonidus – have captured and enslaved, go free. He will let them return to their countries. And more important, he will let them recover the temple goods – the gods, the statues, the ceremonial vessels that had been confiscated. The peoples whom the Babylonians had oppressed and deported may go home, and they may take with them their temple goods and their gods.

In short, they will be allowed to restore their altars and to worship their gods in their own way, in their own place. This decree, this Cylinder is the archaeological evidence for the biblical story

Adriaen Collaert,
Cyrus Maior, 1575–1618,
engraving, 22.0 x 26.1 cm.
British Museum, London (1948,0410.4.58)

that the Jews, after exile in Babylon, after years spent by the waters of Babylon, weeping when they remembered Zion, were to be allowed to go home. They might return to Jerusalem and rebuild the Temple.

It is a defining moment in Jewish history, told in the Book of Chronicles and the Book of Ezra. Here is the Hebrew scriptures' version of the same royal decree. 'Thus said Cyrus, king of Persia, "All the kingdoms of the earth has the Lord God of heaven given me, and he has charged me to build him a house in Jerusalem. Who is there among you of his people? The Lord God be with him, and let him go up."' As is well known, that going up, that return from exile, to rebuild the Temple, reshaped Judaism. And that great historic event was made possible by Cyrus, the king of Persia, reported for us in Hebrew and Aramaic in the Bible and in Babylonian in clay.

Two great texts: what about the politics? The Persian conquest of Babylon marked a fundamental shift in Middle Eastern history. The empire of Iran, of the Medes and the Persians united under Cyrus, became the first great world empire, ultimately controlling the whole of the eastern Mediterranean. This empire, in fact, created the Middle East as we now know it, the area running from Libya and Turkey in the west to the borders of Afghanistan in the East (see map on p. 26). It was the largest empire the world had known until then, an unprecedentedly diverse state on such a huge scale. In consequence, it had to be run in a quite new way and run in several different languages. It had to recognize different peoples, their different habits and different faiths.

Cyrus invented a model of how to run a multilingual, multifaith, multicultural society. Of course this empire was held together by military force, but it was governed on principles so tolerant of diversity that it provided 200 years of stability for the region until it was shattered by the aggression of Alexander. Alexander's successors could not sustain his conquests and the empire fragmented. But what Cyrus had created lived on – a dream of the Middle East as a coherent unit, in which people of different faiths could live together. It was an ideal even his enemies admired.

The Greek historian Xenophon wrote his book *Cyropaedia* acknowledging Cyrus as a great, exemplary ruler. Throughout European culture in consequence, Cyrus remained a model for princes.

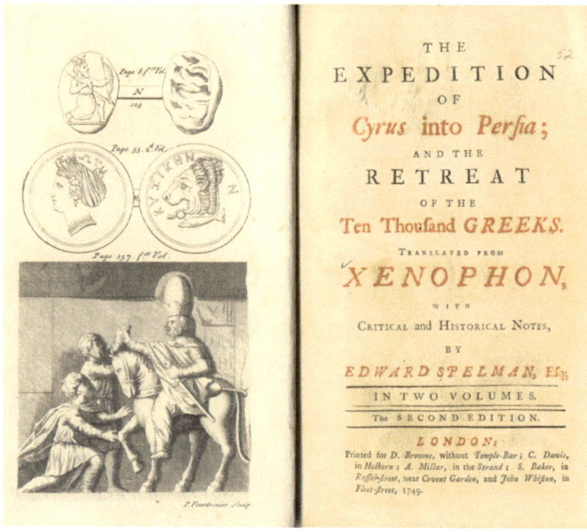

THE
EXPEDITION
OF
Cyrus into *Persia*;
AND THE
RETREAT
OF THE
Ten Thousand *GREEKS*.
TRANSLATED FROM
XENOPHON,
WITH
CRITICAL and HISTORICAL NOTES,
BY
EDWARD SPELMAN, Esq;
IN TWO VOLUMES.
The SECOND EDITION.
LONDON:
Printed for *D. Browne*, without *Temple-Bar*; *C. Davis*, in *Holborn*; *A. Millar*, in the *Strand*; *S. Baker*, in *Russel-street*, near *Covent Garden*, and *John Whiston*, in *Fleet-street*, 1749.

Title page of Xenophon's *Cyropaedia* from the collection of Thomas Jefferson's personal books in the Library of Congress, Washington (Sowerby 20, Jefferson Collection).

The engraving by the sixteenth-century Flemish artist Adriaen Collaert shows how widespread this veneration was in Renaissance Europe. Xenophon's book on Cyrus, on how a diverse society might be managed, remained popular well into the Enlightenment, inspiring the Founding Fathers of the American Revolution. Jefferson was an admirer – the ideals of Cyrus obviously chimed harmoniously with eighteenth-century notions of religious tolerance in a complex state.

But by the eighteenth century, Babylon itself was in a sorry state. Conquered many times, and reduced to ruins, the city had all but vanished from sight. European archaeologists began searching for remains, and in 1879 the Cylinder was discovered by a British Museum expedition. At this point it enters a different story, that great nineteenth-century debate over the reliability of the Judaeo-Christian scriptures. Until 1879 we knew about the return of the Jews and the decree of Cyrus only from the Hebrew scriptures. There was no other evidence. To a world where the authority of scripture had been shaken by arguments over evolution and geology, here, apparently, was proof that the scriptures were in some parts historically, verifiably true.

But if the facts now seemed certain, their interpretation was rather less secure, because the Cylinder account and the Hebrew Bible account differ in one key respect. Cyrus's conquest was a military triumph and God, we know, is usually on the side of the big battalions. The question is, which god? The Babylonian Cylinder is written by the priests of the great god of Babylon, Marduk. And, not surprisingly, they report that Cyrus's heroic deeds were ordained and guided by – Marduk. Marduk, we are told, called Cyrus by his name, took Cyrus by the hand, called him to shepherd his people and gave him the rule of Babylon. Marduk told Cyrus that he should do these great, generous things and set the enslaved peoples free.

The Hebrew writers in the Old Testament, unsurprisingly, take a rather different view. For them, of course, it cannot possibly be Marduk who made all this happen. It could only be Jehovah. And so in Isaiah, we find the rousing passage giving all the credit for this, not to Marduk, but to the Lord God of Israel – who also called Cyrus by name, also took Cyrus by the hand and talks of him shepherding his people. It is a remarkable, unsettling example of two different priestly appropriations of the same

Gold coin, 1 Pahlavi, issued by the Shah of Iran in 1971.
Obverse: Mohammed Reza Shah Pahlavi
Reverse: Cyrus Cylinder.
British Museum, London (1972,0816.1).

military event, two different religious readings of the same political fact.

The Cyrus Cylinder, like the Mesopotamian tablet with the story of the Flood, deciphered in the British Museum in 1878, made it uncomfortably clear that the Hebrew scriptures take their place in a much wider world of Levantine religions. The Cylinder is older than the text of Isaiah, and yet, Jehovah speaks in words very similar to those used by Marduk. There is a sense that Isaiah grasps the complexity of all this, because he reports Jehovah saying to Cyrus, 'I have called thee by thy name though thou hast not known me.' Ironically it is unlikely that Cyrus would have recognized either Jehovah or Marduk. His own understanding of god would have been – of course – an Iranian one, perhaps a Zoroastrian one.

It is impossible to know whether the Jewish and Babylonian writers are merely attributing to their own gods the actions of the king, or whether the Persians themselves encouraged the different peoples to see Cyrus as enjoying the particular protection of the many deities of the empire. Perhaps the most likely explanation of the similarity of language is that Jewish scribes working in the Babylonian administration transmitted the wording to Jerusalem. We await further evidence which might resolve the question.

Nearly forty years after its discovery, in 1917, the Cylinder once again entered a different world. 1917 was the year of the Balfour Declaration, when the new imperial power in the Middle East, Great Britain, declared that it would establish a Jewish national home, allowing the Jews to return to Israel. The response of much of the Jewish population of Eastern Europe was enthusiastic. In his book *The Palestine Triangle*, the historian Nicholas Bethell writes that in Eastern Europe, Jews displayed images of Cyrus and of George V side by side – the two great emperors who allowed the Jews to return to Zion. Cyrus now comes back into public view, his political resonance renewed and enlarged. The model ruler of the Enlightenment is seen as very much a man for the twentieth century, the first Prime Minister of Israel, David Ben Gurion, describing him as displaying 'a spirit of charity towards his adversaries, and a unique tolerance towards all religions.' Cyrus had become a Zionist hero.

Prime Minister Ben Gurion was not alone in his admiration. Mohammad Reza Pahlavi, the Shah of Iran, also revered Cyrus – in his case as the founder of the Persian monarchy and the accepted leader of the ancient Near East. When the Shah held his famous celebrations at Persepolis in 1971, to mark the 2,500th anniversary of

Photographers at the opening ceremony of the Cyrus Cylinder exhibition in the National Museum of Iran, September 2010.

the Iranian throne, he addressed Cyrus as his great precursor. He asked the British Museum to lend the Cyrus Cylinder to Tehran as part of the festivities, and its presence in Iran was commemorated by the striking of a gold medal showing the Shah on one side, and the Cyrus Cylinder on the other. The coin was part of an extensive campaign to present the Shah as the direct heir to Cyrus, valiant in his defence of Iran, and benign in his impact on the surrounding nations. It was powerful political messaging.

So it was not surprising that the Islamic revolution of 1979, having expelled the Shah, initially turned its back on Cyrus and the proud imperial story. The association of Cyrus with the Shah was too disquieting, and the focus of the new Islamic Republic was of course on Iran's later, Islamic history. Until, that is, the Iran–Iraq War broke out, in 1980, with Saddam Hussein, the enthusiastic restorer of Nebuchadnezzar's Babylon, the principal aggressor.

Then it became critical for Iranians to remember their great past, the moment when they had heroically fought Iraq and won. It was important also to find a symbol that would pull together all Iranians – Muslims and non-Muslims, Christians, Zoroastrians and Jews. And one obvious emblem of national cohesion was Cyrus.

The British Museum and Tehran National Museum have long cooperated and worked together. Many great loans have come from Iran to London. In return, the Iranians asked to borrow the Cyrus Cylinder. And in 2010, in spite of political tensions, the Cylinder went to Tehran for the second time to be the focus of a special exhibition at the National Museum. It was a huge event, visited by around half a million people in the space of a few months. This is a figure comparable to any blockbuster show in the West. The exhibition sparked serious debate about what this Cylinder now means, what Cyrus now means, but above all, about Cyrus as articulated through this Cylinder – defender of the homeland, champion of Iranian identity and of the Iranian people, tolerant of all faiths. It was pointed out that this tradition is still enshrined in the current Iranian constitution, which reserves places in parliament for a Christian (Armenian), a Zoroastrian and a Jew. And while the Cylinder was on show, many Jews living in Iran came to Tehran to see it.

In the opening ceremony of the exhibition, President Mahmoud Ahmadinejad reminded the audience of the challenges which the Cyrus Cylinder poses to modern Iran. Is Iran still to be the defender of the oppressed? Will Iran set

free the people that tyrants have enslaved and expropriated? It was heady national rhetoric, all part of a colourful pageant, in which great figures from Iranian history gathered round an outsized Cyrus Cylinder, all participants in the long epic of Iranian national identity.

To accompany this object to Iran was to witness an extraordinary debate led at the highest political levels about what Iran is, and how the different histories of Iran might shape the world today. It is a debate that is still continuing, because this object is one of the great expressions of a long human aspiration. It bears comparison with the American constitution in spite of the centuries that divide them, as an historic statement of how a disparate polity may be humanely governed. And it is fitting that a replica of the Cyrus Cylinder is on permanent display in the United Nations building.

I want to finish by asking you, the reader, what the next story might be in which this object will figure. Is there a chance that it could be the story of a Middle East governed by the principles asserted in the Cyrus Cylinder? A Middle East based on the right of different peoples to live together in the same state, worshipping differently, and freely – a Middle East, a world, in which religion is not the subject of division or dispute?

In the Middle East at the moment, debates are often, we all know, shrill. But I think it is possible that the wisest voice of all of them may well be the voice of this mute and broken piece of clay, the Cyrus Cylinder.

This essay is based on the TED lecture given by Neil MacGregor, Edinburgh, July 2011. A full transcript and video can be found at http://www.ted.com/talks/neil_macgregor_2600_years_of_history_in_one_object.html

(above left) President Mahmoud Ahmadinejad at the opening ceremony of the Cyrus Cylinder exhibition in the National Museum of Iran, September 2010.

(above right) A large-scale version of the Cyrus Cylinder on stage as part of a pageant celebrating Iranian history and culture to mark the visit of the Cyrus Cylinder to Iran in 2010.

Introduction

This exhibition has been put together around the Cyrus Cylinder, one of the most famous icons to have survived from the ancient world and one of the most significant objects now in the British Museum. The Cylinder was inscribed in Babylonian cuneiform on the orders of the Persian king Cyrus the Great after he captured Babylon in 539 BC. It describes how Cyrus made himself king of Babylon with the encouragement of the Babylonian god Marduk and went on to return god statues removed from various shrines by the Babylonian kings. Captive peoples were also to be allowed to return with the god statues. Although the Jews are not mentioned in the Cylinder, it is thought to be at this time that they returned to Jerusalem to build the second temple, as recorded in 2 Chronicles and Ezra-Nehemiah. Because of these apparently enlightened acts by Cyrus, the Cylinder has been regarded as an innovative document and has even been referred to as the First Bill of Human Rights. Such claims are clearly an exaggeration, and presuppose that the concept of human rights existed in the ancient world, which it did not. Nevertheless, the Cylinder shows Cyrus in a different light to other Middle Eastern conquerors and this is borne out by the biblical and classical traditions. The Cylinder may fairly be said to mark a break with the past, and it ushered in two centuries of Persian rule in the region.

Under Darius the Great (522–486 BC) the Persian empire reached its greatest size, extending from Egypt to India and from Arabia to the Aral Sea. There were even excursions into Greece, but after the Greco-Persian Wars the western frontier of the empire was effectively at the Dardanelles. Nevertheless, this was a vast territory to administer, being substantially larger than any empire the world had seen up until that time, and to do so effectively new practices and different ways of doing things were introduced. There were also technological advances during this time, as well as artistic and architectural developments. From many points of view, therefore, the Persian period may be described as a new beginning for the Middle East. The objects that accompany the Cylinder have been chosen to reflect this. Thus, there are inscriptions in the newly introduced Old Persian cuneiform, new and wonderful forms of jewellery and tableware and a gold plaque from the Oxus Treasure that shows a priest who is probably Zoroastrian. Coins began to be widely circulated at this time, and the Aramaic language and script was widely used for communication. With seals there was a reversal to traditional types, such as the famous cylinder seal of Darius. All in all, this was a period of Middle Eastern history that has been much denigrated in the past and only now is the contribution that it made beginning to be properly appreciated.

Arrangements for this travelling exhibition have been made by Clare Eardley, Jill Maggs and Dean Baylis and they have liaised with the US venues and with representatives of the Iran Heritage Foundation who have sponsored the tour. We are most grateful to the IHF for their interest in this project and for their help and support. Sarah Faulks and Carolyn Jones of British Museum Press have been most helpful in preparing this volume for publication.

1 Tomb of Xerxes (486–465 BC) at Naqsh-i Rustam near Persepolis.

Chapter I

The Origins of the Persians

When people speaking Indo-European languages arrived on the Iranian plateau they came into contact with civilizations that were already old. In the south-western part of Iran, Elamite civilization had flourished since at least 3000 BC and had its own language and distinctive cuneiform writing system. In the south-east of the country, sites such as Shahdad, Tepe Yahya and Jiroft were part of a vast trading network that around 2500 BC extended from Mesopotamia far into Central Asia. In the west of Iran, along the foothills of the Zagros Mountains, there were communities that had thrived since Neolithic times, benefitting from the rich agricultural resources of the countryside.

The origins of these Indo-European tribes and the manner of their arrival in Iran are subjects that are still hotly debated. There are two principal schools of thought about the birthplace of the Indo-European language family. One theory localizes this phenomenon in the steppes to the north of the Black Sea, while the other would place it in western Turkey (Anatolia), believing that the languages spread with the expansion of farming, wheeled vehicles and horses. Another candidate for the possible homeland must surely be in the heart of what we now call Central Asia. A recent article in the prestigious journal *Science* claims that new linguistic analysis conclusively demonstrates that the Indo-European language family originated in Anatolia, but no doubt counter-arguments will be forthcoming. However this may be, the traditional view is that migrants in this case speaking Indo-Iranian languages started to arrive on the Iranian plateau soon after 2000 BC, having travelled down the east side of the Caspian Sea. Amongst these peoples would have been tribes who later came to be identified as the Medes and the Persians, and it is believed that most modern Iranians, or at least their Indo-European Persian language, are descended from these early immigrants. This is an attractive and convenient theory, but difficult to verify. It is particularly unclear how many people may have been involved in these early migrations, but DNA research would suggest that the numbers were quite small; a recent study, based on 938 samples, apparently points to 'an autochthonous non-homogeneous ancient Y-chromosome gene pool'. In other words, successive migrations from the Neolithic period onwards have not substantially altered the basic make up of the population (fig. 2).

Even if their number were small, however, the Indo-European immigrants made a major impact, and by the early first millennium BC we have documentary evidence for both the Medes and the Persians in western Iran. The Medes are first mentioned in the records of their powerful western neighbours, the Assyrians, in the reign

2 Map showing ancient and modern sites and settlements in the central part of the ancient Persian Empire.

of Shalmaneser III (858–824 BC), and for the next 200 years they were to be a thorn in the side of the Assyrians. The Medes and the Assyrians frequently clashed, and the Assyrians encountered the Medes in a series of military campaigns into the Zagros region and beyond. Representations of campaigns against the Medes, notably during the reigns of Tiglath-pileser III (744–727 BC) and Sargon (721–705 BC) were shown on the stone wall reliefs in Assyrian palaces. These carvings

3 (facing page) View of Tepe Nush-i Jan in 1996 with a modern roof protecting the central part of the site.

feature Median fortresses with towers and crenellated battlements. So-called 'vassal-treaties' from the reign of the Assyrian king Esarhaddon (680–669 BC) show that by this time the Medes had become a serious threat to Assyria, which was then the most powerful state in the Ancient Near East. These clay tablets found at Nimrud in Assyria record agreements between the Medes and the Assyrians in which the Medes promise to recognize the succession to the Assyrian throne. This may have given the Assyrians some security for the next fifty years or so, but at the end of the 7th century BC, in the years 614–612 BC, under their king Cyaxares, the Medes teamed up with the Babylonians to launch a series of attacks on Assyria. The coup de grâce was delivered in 612 BC, when all the major Assyrian cities, including Nineveh and Nimrud, were sacked and destroyed. The scale of this devastation was unprecedented, and at all the Assyrian cities deep deposits of ash and burnt debris bear witness to the intensity of the destruction. This sequence of events gave the Medes a footing on what was then the world stage, and the free run of what had previously been the Assyrian heartland in northern Mesopotamia brought them into conflict with the powerful Lydian kingdom in western and central Turkey. Five years of warfare beginning in 590 BC culminated in a famous battle in 585 BC that was dramatically interrupted by a solar eclipse. Peace was made, and the frontier between Lydia and the Medes was established on the River Halys. In the east, Median conquests are difficult to document, but the Medes probably advanced at least as far as the River Oxus (Amu Darya) in Central Asia. By the middle of the 6th century BC, therefore, the Medes were loosely in control of a vast swathe of territory extending from the Halys to the Oxus.

In spite of references to the Medes in the Assyrian and Babylonian records, however, our information about them is tantalizingly inadequate. The Greek historian Herodotus includes a long account about the Medes in his *Histories*, but this is generally regarded as unreliable by modern historians. Part of the problem is that traces of the Medes in the archaeological record are meagre. There is just a handful of archaeological sites in Iran that have been identified as Median, or having Median levels, including Tepe Nush-i Jan (fig. 3) near Hamadan, Godin Tepe near Kangavar, Baba Jan in Luristan and perhaps Tepe Ozbaki about 75 km north-west of Tehran. Even Hamadan, which according to the classical authors Herodotus and Polybius was the main centre of Median power, has failed up until now to yield any evidence of Median presence. Yet, to cite an often-quoted archaeological dictum, we should not see absence of evidence as evidence of absence. Although it is true that Hamadan may not be mentioned in

the Assyrian sources (this is disputed), it is certain that in the early Achaemenid period (see p. 23) Hamadan was an important place. Thus, it is recorded in the Babylonian document known as the Nabonidus Chronicle that after Cyrus had defeated Astyages, the last Median king, he captured Ecbatana (Hamadan) and carried off valuable booty to Anshan. In the Bisitun inscription Darius says that he executed Phraortes and the Median nobles who had rebelled with him at Hamadan, which was clearly viewed then as the most important centre in Media. It seems clear, then, that at least in the last part of the pre-Achaemenid period, Hamadan must have been an important Median centre.

Nevertheless, the lack of evidence about the Medes has led many authorities to conclude that the Medes were merely a loose confederation of tribes who had little if any centralized structure and cannot be considered as a 'state' in the modern sense of the word. For example, it has been questioned whether a discrete and united Median kingdom can be postulated much before 615 BC. Part of the problem is the absence of any Median records. As far as we know, the Medes were illiterate, and, so the argument goes, the Medes could not have been masters of a complex state organization if they did not have access to proper recording systems. However, we would do well to remember that we do not have much evidence of how state business was recorded in the early Achaemenid period. Cyrus himself may well have written in Elamite, and Aramaic may have been in quite extensive use, but the Old Persian language and script were only used (and then from the time of Darius) for monumental inscriptions and there are no extensive archives in an Iranian language. In these circumstances, it would seem wise to reserve judgement for the time being about the nature of the Median state.

A similar problem afflicts studies of Median art. Some scholars have identified many splendid objects as the products of Median artists and craftsmen, while others have denied that any objects can be labelled as examples of Median art. The truth probably lies somewhere between these two extremes, and further research and discoveries will surely in due course allow us to establish a canon of Median art and material culture. In the meantime, a few general observations may be made. The Apadana reliefs at Persepolis show the Median delegation bringing offerings consisting of items that were presumably at that time (in the early Achaemenid period) considered to be typical Median products. They comprise vessels probably in precious metal, a short sword (*akinakes*), bracelets and folded costumes probably of the same type as the delegates are wearing, namely trouser suits with hoods. Further evidence from the Achaemenid period in the form of Darius' foundation inscription at Susa indicates that the Medes were skilled at wall decoration, whatever that may exactly have been. Although they are later, these sources provide us with a glimpse of the sorts of arts and crafts that may have flourished in the late Median period. The evidence from the so-called Median sites themselves is sparse, but finds from Tepe Nush-i Jan seem to show, as might be expected, that there was an element of Assyrian influence in Median material culture.

If the prehistory of the Medes is contradictory and elusive, that of the Persians is even more so. The name Parsua as a district in the Zagros region is first attested in the time of Shalmaneser III (858–824 BC), but although there is presumably a link between the names, in that the Persians gave their name to the district or took it from the district, we cannot be sure that they were there at that time. A further complication is that the location of Parsua shifts over time. However this may be, as we shall see below by the 6th century BC the Persians were well established in Fars province with their centre at Anshan, a formerly Elamite stronghold. From this base they were able, in conjunction with the Medes, to launch an empire that dominated the Middle East for more than 200 years.

Chapter II

History of the Persian Empire

According to the Greek authors, on whom we are much reliant for a reconstruction of early Persian history, Cyrus was the son of Cambyses, king of Persia and Mandane, the daughter of the Median king Astyages. He was therefore the grandson of Astyages, whom he defeated in battle in 550 BC, thereby uniting the houses of Persia and Media. In this way, Cyrus came into possession of all the territory previously controlled by the Medes. So began what is often called the Achaemenid period, named after the eponymous founder of the dynasty, Achaemenes. Cyrus went on to defeat Croesus of Lydia in 547 or 546, which brought much of central and western Turkey under his control. Then in 539 BC, as described in the Cyrus Cylinder, he conquered Babylon. The Cylinder claims that he entered Babylon 'without fighting or battle', which may be a slight exaggeration as both Herodotus and Xenophon relate that his troops could only get access to the city by diverting the River Euphrates and wading along its bed, but they do not refer to any subsequent violence or looting (Herodotus, *Histories* I, 190–2; Xenophon, *Cyropaedia* VII, v. 7–34). The capture of Babylon added to the possessions of Cyrus the former Babylonian empire, extending to the Mediterranean Sea. To the east, he is thought to have campaigned as far as the Aral Sea. Cyrus built for himself a new city at Pasargadae, in Fars province in south-west Iran, and when he died in 530 BC he was buried there in a splendid stone tomb (fig. 21).

He was succeeded by his son Cambyses, who successfully invaded Egypt and officially adopted the titles and costume of the pharaohs, although according to Greek sources he clashed with the Egyptian priesthood. At the end of Cambyses' reign there was a period of unrest that culminated in the seizure of the throne by Darius the Great (522–486 BC). According to the account of Darius in his inscription at Bisitun (figs 6 and 7), Cambyses had had a brother named Bardiya whom he murdered. While Cambyses was in Egypt a revolt broke out, headed by a Magian (a priest) called Gaumata (in Greek sources the false Smerdis), claiming that he was Bardiya. Cambyses died while he was on his way back from Egypt to quell the revolt, which seems to been nothing short of a civil war in which Darius was victorious. Darius immediately set about establishing his credentials to the throne. In the Bisitun inscription he says: 'My father was Hystaspes; Hystaspes' father was Arsames; Arsames' father was Ariaramnes; Ariaramnes' father was Teispes; Teispes' father was Achaemenes…For this reason we are called Achaemenians…From long ago our family had been kings.'

The significance of this statement becomes clear when we consider what Cyrus says about his ancestry in the Cyrus Cylinder:

4 A cuneiform tablet with a text in Elamite and a seal impression showing a spearman on a horse fighting against three enemies, two of whom are dead. The inscription to the left of the impression reads 'Kurash the Anshanite, son of Teispes', who may have been the grandfather of Cyrus the Great. National Museum of Iran.

5 Drawing of the seal impression of Kurash, son of Teispes.

> I am Cyrus, king of the universe, the great king, the powerful king, king of Babylon, king of Sumer and Akkad, king of the four quarters of the world, son of Cambyses, the great king, king of the city of Anshan, grandson of Cyrus, the great king, ki[ng of the ci]ty of Anshan, descendant of Teispes, the great king, king of the city of Anshan [figs 4 and 5].

Darius, then, traces his ancestry back to Teispes who was also an ancestor of Cyrus, and Darius provides the extra information that Teispes was the son of Achaemenes. If it is true what Darius says, then he would have belonged to what was effectively a separate branch of the Achaemenid royal family. He would actually have been the third cousin of Cambyses. However, most authorities believe that Darius was an impostor and that his genealogy was fabricated. It was to strengthen his claim, they argue, that Darius wrote inscriptions at Pasargadae saying 'I am Cyrus the king, an Achaemenian'. Also, it is curious that there should have been Achaemenid kings both in Anshan (Cyrus and his predecessors) and Parsa, the district around Persepolis (Darius and his predecessors), when Anshan, now identified as Tall-i Malyan, is only 50 km north-west of Persepolis.

Darius left for posterity a record of the events at the beginning of his reign at Bisitun (figs 6 and 7) on the highway between Hamadan and Kermanshah. High on a cliff-face overlooking the road he engraved a panel commemorating his victory over Gaumata and nine rebel kings. The kings are shown roped together at the neck in front of Darius, while Gaumata lies under his feet. Hovering above the scene is the figure in the winged disc, probably Ahuramazda or the kingly glory. The relief is accompanied by three long inscriptions giving the same version of events in Elamite, Old Persian and Babylonian.

In spite of this controversial beginning, Darius went on to achieve great things. Under him the Persian empire reached its greatest extent, stretching from North Africa to the Indus Valley and from Central Asia to the Persian Gulf (fig. 8). He is credited with being a brilliant administrator who refined the organization of the empire into provinces, each under the charge

6 The rock relief of Darius at Bisitun, carved in 520–519 BC. Darius has his foot on the prostrate Gaumata (the false Smerdis) and in front of him are the nine rebel kings, roped together. There are lengthy cuneiform inscriptions in Old Persian, Elamite and Babylonian, and the copying of these inscriptions by Henry Creswicke Rawlinson in the 19th century greatly helped in the decipherment of cuneiform.

7 (bottom) Drawing of the rock relief at Bisitun published by the British Museum in 1907. The epigraphs are written in Old Persian (Per.), Elamite (Sus.) and Babylonian (Bab.).

of a satrap or provincial governor, and improved communications around the empire, such as the so-called 'royal road' from Susa to Sardis. In the time of Darius, Old Persian cuneiform was introduced for writing inscriptions in the Old Persian language (see cat. no. 5) and coins were produced in the royal mint (see cat. nos 8–9). It is also from the time of Darius onwards that we have royal inscriptions extolling Ahuramazda. In line with his territorial ambitions, Darius was also an energetic builder. He launched at least two grandiose building programmes, notably at Susa and Persepolis.

The end of Darius' reign is marked by the beginning of the conflicts with Greece that are known to history as the Greco-Persian Wars. Trouble began when the Ionians in Asia Minor revolted and sacked Sardis. The revolt was suppressed, but the Ionians had been supported by Athens as well as Eretria on the island of

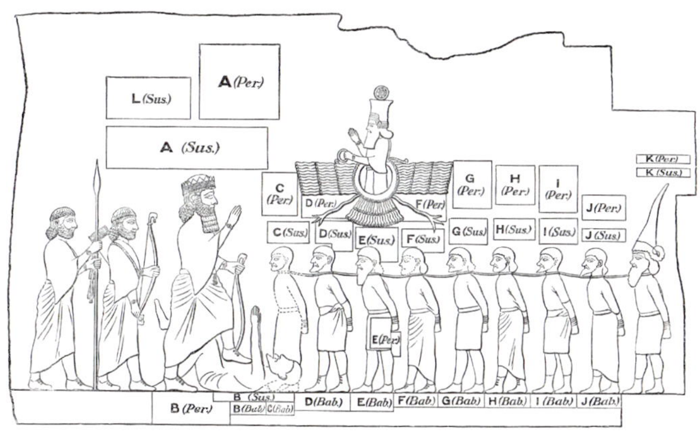

Euboea. Darius saw this as a reason to invade mainland Greece. In their first invasion of Greece, in 490 BC, the Persians succeeded in capturing Eretria but suffered a reverse at the Battle of Marathon.

There was then a cessation of hostilities until the reign of Xerxes (486–465 BC), who in 480 BC launched a second invasion. After defeating a Greek force commanded by Leonidas of Sparta at the Pass of Thermopylae in Central Greece,

8 Map of the Persian Empire at its greatest extent showing the principal provinces and the route of the royal road from Susa to Sardis.

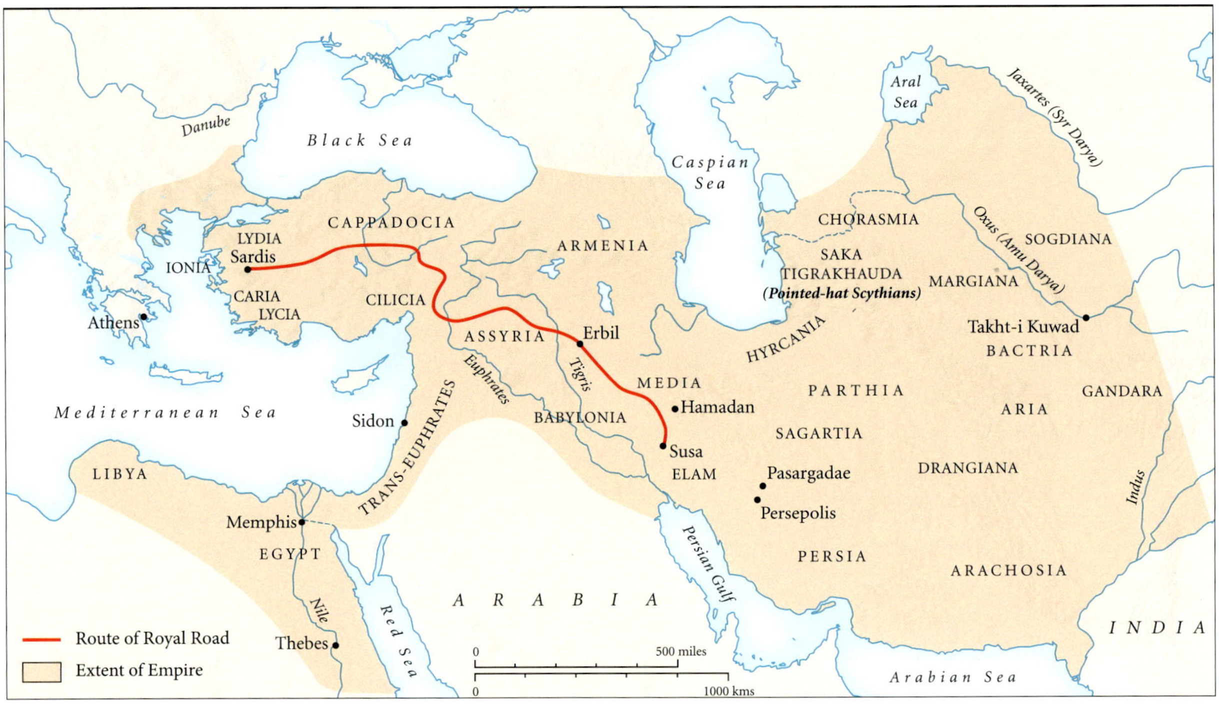

the Persians advanced on Athens and sacked and burned the city. Following this there was a naval engagement in the Straits of Salamis which, had they won it, would have allowed the Persians to march into the Peloponnese. However, the Persian navy suffered a heavy defeat at Salamis, and the following year the Persian army under Mardonius, who had been left behind by Xerxes to complete the conquest, was routed at Plataea. This, and another naval defeat at Mycale, signalled the end of the Persian attempt to overrun Greece. Much has been written about the Greco-Persian Wars, and absurd claims have been made about a supposed victory of democracy over despotism. The fact is that everything we know about the conflict comes from Greek sources; the Persian sources are silent, and we do not know if it was ever the intention of the Persian kings to add Greece to their empire. Even the Greek sources indicate that the purpose of the invasion was punitive, to punish the Athenians and Eretrians for sending troops to help Ionia in their revolt against Persia, and if this was indeed the motive it had the desired results. There was never again an attempt by mainland Greek states to interfere in Asia Minor.

Like his father Darius, Xerxes was a great builder who continued with the construction programme at Persepolis (fig. 9). His reign was marred, however, by intrigues, such as that recorded in the Book of Esther, and Xerxes was eventually assassinated. This was a recurring theme, and the succession was often disputed. For example, at the beginning of the reign of Artaxerxes II (404–359 BC) his brother, known as Cyrus the Younger, made a bid for the throne, but

9 View of the Persepolis terrace seen from the slopes of the neighbouring mountain, looking west.

was defeated at Cunaxa, north of Babylon. Cyrus' army included 10,000 Greek mercenaries, one of whom, Xenophon, left a record of his experiences in his *Anabasis*. There were also a number of rebellions in the Achaemenid period, and Egypt was able to regain its independence for about sixty years from 400 until 343/2 BC. In spite of all this, both Artaxerxes II and Artaxerxes III (359–338 BC) in particular engaged in building projects, and there is no real evidence for economic or social decline before the end of the Achaemenid period. The apparent ease with which Alexander the Great was able to conquer the empire is therefore difficult to explain. Pierre Briant suggests that the Macedonians were tactically and strategically superior, but even if they were it is tempting to seek other reasons. One possibility is that Alexander was able to win the support of some provincial officials and perhaps even some courtiers.

Alexander's conquest of the Near East started in 334 BC. In that year he crossed the Hellespont with his Macedonian army, and the armies of the last Achaemenid king Darius III (336–331 BC) were defeated first at the River Granicus, then at Issus and finally at Gaugamela in northern Iraq in 331 BC. He eventually burned Persepolis, an act of cultural vandalism for which the Iranians have never forgiven him, but not before he had looted Susa. He entered the city without a struggle, and proceeded to empty the royal treasury. This event is graphically described by a number of classical authors including Arrian in his *Anabasis of Alexander*.

Catalogue: Part 1

A New Code of Ethical Behaviour

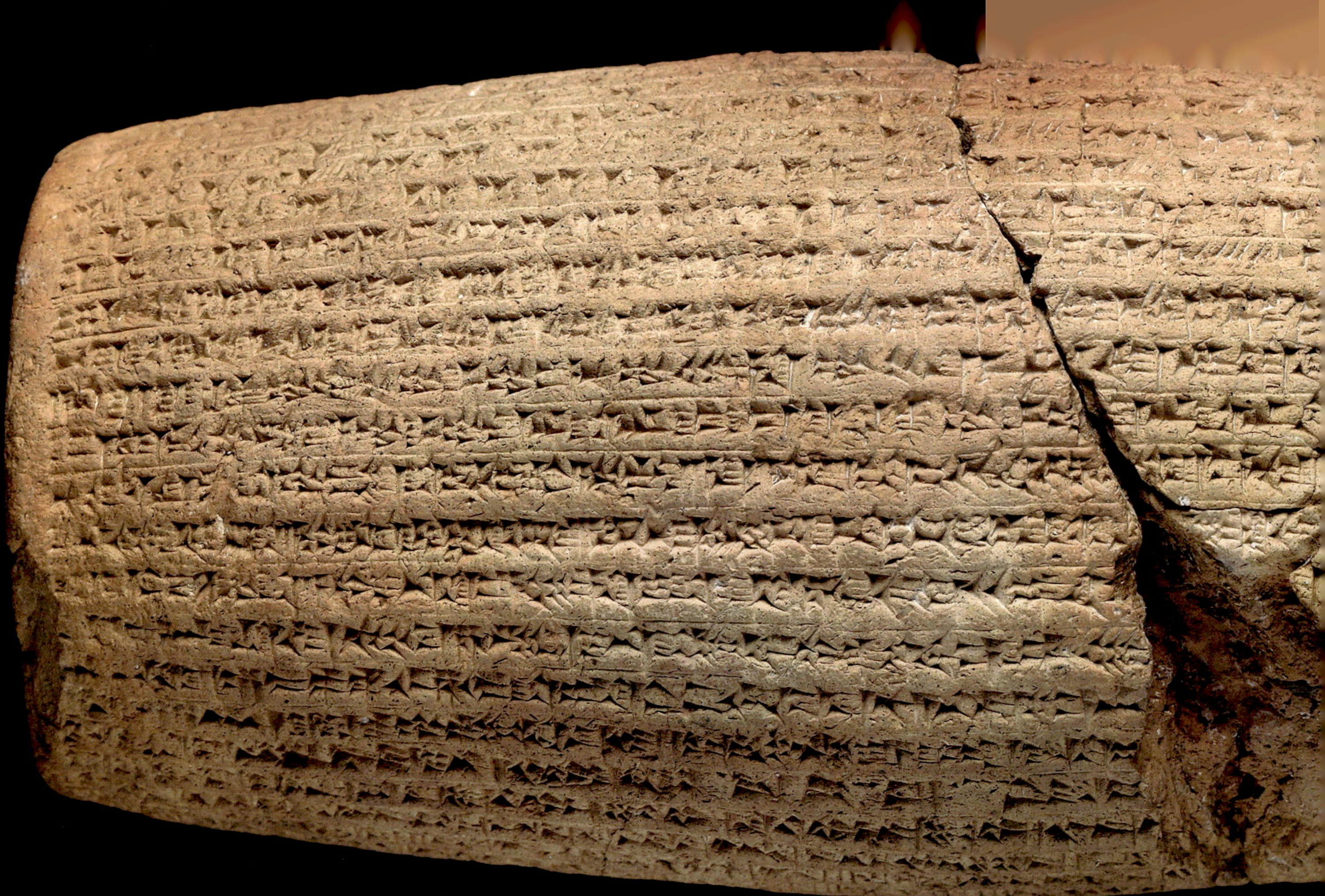

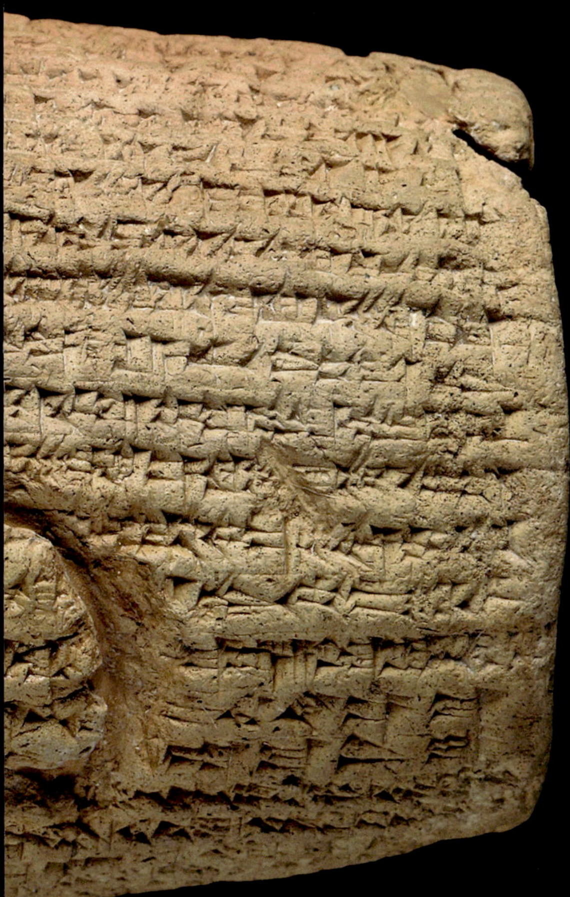

1 # The Cyrus Cylinder

539–538 BC, Achaemenid Period
Excavated in Babylon in 1879
Baked clay

L. 22.86 cm, diam. 10.0 cm
BM 90920 (1880,0617.1941)

The Cyrus Cylinder is a barrel-shaped clay cylinder that is Persian inscribed in Babylonian cuneiform characters (wedge-shaped script). It was written after Cyrus captured Babylon in 539 BC and was buried as a foundation deposit. It was customary for Babylonian and Assyrian kings to bury inscribed clay cylinders of this kind under new buildings as foundation deposits, so Cyrus was following an ancient tradition. The cylinders usually record the achievements of the kings in question and seek protection from particular gods. In this case, the Cylinder describes the conquest of Babylon by Cyrus, his returning of god statues and his (restoration) work at Babylon. Much is made in the Cylinder of the awfulness of the previous king of Babylon, Nabonidus, who is described as 'a low person'. In fact, it is clear from Babylonian sources that Nabonidus was certainly deficient in his kingly role: he promoted worship of the moon god Sin at the expense of Marduk, the chief Babylonian god, and for a period of ten years he resided at Teima, in present-day Saudi Arabia, where he built a temple dedicated to the moon god. During his absence from Babylon his son Belshazzar (Bel-sharra-usur) acted as regent, but in that capacity he could not substitute for the king in important religious ceremonies such as the New Year (*akitu*) Festival, which had to be abandoned.

The Cylinder was apparently broken, either accidentally or even deliberately, at the time of its discovery or soon after, and is made up of several pieces that have been fixed together. A small joining fragment (8.6 x 5.6 cm) preserving part of lines 36–45 of the text, belonging to Yale University (NBC 2504), was identified in 1971, but just over one-third of the Cylinder is still missing. The Yale fragment is part of a collection of tablets acquired by the Revd Dr James B. Nies from dealers in Baghdad, Europe and the United States between 1905 and 1920 and presented by him to Yale University.

The text of the Cylinder is written in parallel lines extending from one end of the Cylinder to the other. All or parts of forty-five lines of the text are preserved, while about twenty or more are completely missing. The missing parts include portions of some lines at the beginning and the end of the text. The Cylinder was evidently written by a Babylonian scribe who was familiar with Babylonian textual and literary traditions. The style is Babylonian, and some sentences recall earlier texts of the Neo-Babylonian period (612–539 BC). However, the scribe may have been putting into a Babylonian format content that was determined by the new Persian overlords. The text records that Nabonidus, the last king of Babylon (555–539 BC), had perverted the cults of the Babylonian gods, including Marduk, the city-god of Babylon, and had imposed labour-service on its free population, who complained to the gods. The gods responded by deserting Babylon, but Marduk looked around for a champion to restore the old ways. He chose Cyrus, King of Anshan (in Iran), and declared him king of the world. First Cyrus made the Gutians and the Medes 'prostrate themselves at his feet', and ruled justly over the 'black-headed people'. Then Marduk ordered Cyrus to march on Babylon, which he entered without a fight. Nabonidus was delivered into his hands and the people of Babylon joyfully accepted the kingship of Cyrus. From this point on, the document is written as if Cyrus himself is speaking: 'I, Cyrus, king of the world....' He presents himself as a worshipper of Marduk who brought peace to Babylon and abolished the labour-service of its population. The people of neighbouring countries brought tribute to Babylon, and Cyrus claims to have restored their temples and religious cults, and to have returned their previously deported gods and people. The text ends with a note of additional food offerings in the temples of Babylon and an account of the rebuilding of Imgur-Enlil, the city wall of Babylon, during the course of which an earlier building inscription of Ashurbanipal, King of Assyria (668–627 BC), was found.

The Cyrus Cylinder was found in 1879 at Babylon in modern-day Iraq, then part of the Ottoman empire, during excavations supervised by Hormuzd Rassam (fig. 10) on behalf of the British Museum. Rassam was a native of Mosul

10 Hormuzd Rassam (1826–1910) who was director of the British Museum excavations at Babylon when the Cyrus Cylinder was discovered in 1879.

in northern Iraq, and came from an Assyrian Christian family; his brother Christian Rassam was British Vice-Consul in Mosul. Between 1845 and 1851 Rassam had assisted Austen Henry Layard (later Sir Henry Layard) in his British Museum excavations at Nimrud and Nineveh, and between 1852 and 1854 he had conducted them himself, discovering amongst many other things the famous Assyrian lion hunt reliefs in the North Palace of Ashurbanipal at Nineveh. In 1866–8 he led an ill-fated British mission to Ethiopia to rescue hostages held by Theodore, King of Abyssinia, and then in 1876–82 was persuaded to come out of retirement to undertake further excavations on behalf of the British Museum. A *firman* (permission to excavate) from the Ottoman government was obtained with the help of Sir Henry Layard, who was now Ambassador in Constantinople. This *firman* also allowed Rassam to export any antiquities found to the British Museum (Rassam 1897: p. 259). In this period, Rassam worked at various sites including Balawat in Assyria, where he found the bronze gates of Shalmaneser III (858–824 BC), Toprak Kale near Lake Van in eastern Turkey, where he discovered parts of an Urartian bronze throne, and at Babylon, Sippar and Telloh in Babylonia. From Sippar came the so-called Sun-God Tablet. The Cyrus Cylinder was apparently found at Babylon between February and March 1879, at a time when Rassam himself was not actually at the site.

With regard to the exact find-spot of the Cylinder at Babylon, in a letter to Samuel Birch, Keeper of the Department of Oriental Antiquities at the British Museum, dated 20 November 1879, Rassam wrote, 'The Cylinder of Cyrus was found at Omran with about six hundred pieces of inscribed terracottas [i.e. tablets].' Later, in his *Asshur and the Land of Nimrod* (New York 1897) he wrote on p. 267: 'We discovered in the ruins of

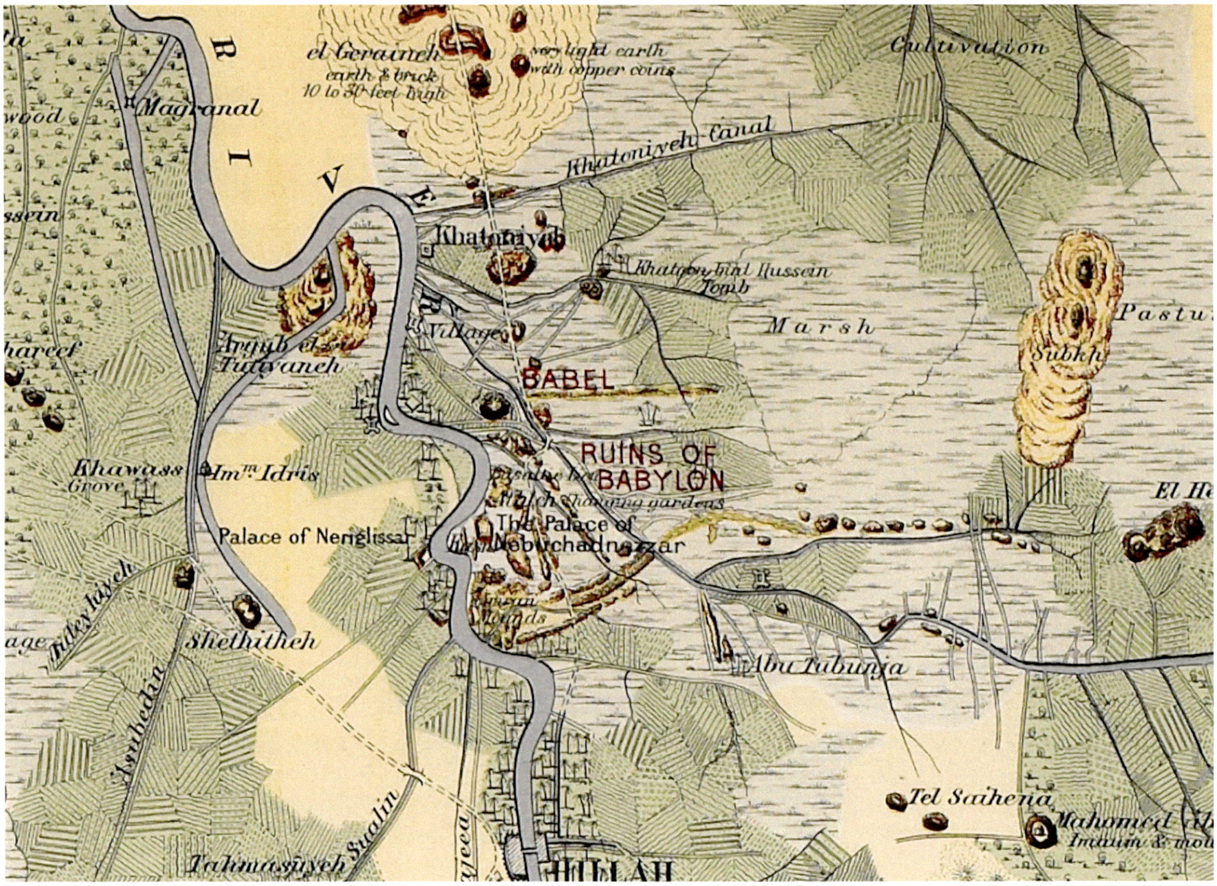

11 Part of map of Babylon and surrounding area published by W.H. Allen & Co., London, in 1885.

12 (facing page) The probable find-spot of the Cyrus Cylinder indicated on Robert Koldewey's plan of Babylon.

Jimjima a broken terra-cotta cylinder, which has been deciphered in the first instance by Sir Henry Rawlinson, and found to contain the official record of the taking of Babylon by Cyrus.' Now, 'Omran' refers to the mound (tell) of Amran ibn Ali, named after the sanctuary on its summit, containing the tomb of Amran son of Ali (figs 11 and 12). In the northern part of the great Amran ibn Ali mound is Esagila, the Temple of Marduk, and the ziggurat (temple tower) named Etemenanki. Jimjima (meaning 'skull' in Arabic) is the name of a village, but the location seems to be indicated rather indiscriminately on different maps. However, Robert Koldewey's map in his book *The Excavations at Babylon* (London 1914) (fig. 12) marks Jimjima near the southern end of Tell Imran ibn Ali, so the two locations given by Rassam are not necessarily in conflict with each other.

Let us now look at the evidence from the Cylinder itself. If it was indeed wholly or partially a building or foundation deposit, the building or feature under which it was buried should be mentioned in the text. This is what Cyrus says: 'I strove to strengthen the defences of the wall Imgur-Enlil, the great wall of Babylon, and [I completed] the quay of baked brick on the bank of the moat which an earlier king had bu[ilt but not com]pleted its work.'

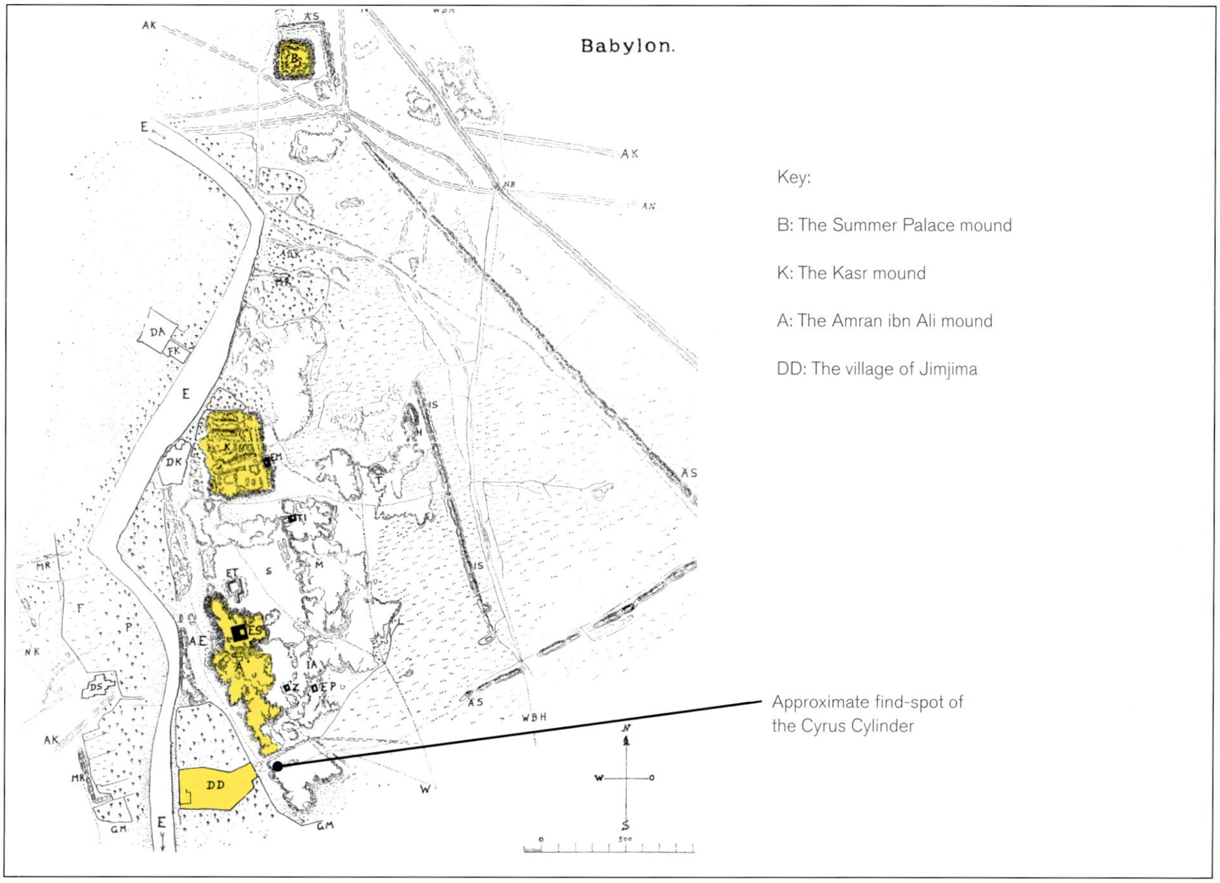

In fact, Imgur-Enlil was the name given to the inner city wall of Babylon, which ran just to the south of the Imran ibn Ali mound. The quay wall could also have been close to this location, bearing in mind that the ancient bed of the Euphrates was to the east of its present course and skirted the western edge of the Imran ibn Ali mound. So, a find-spot at the south or south-west end of the Imran ibn Ali mound, possibly under the inner city wall or the quay wall, or at the junction of the two, seems plausible (fig. 12).

After its arrival in the British Museum in August 1879 the Cylinder was identified by Theophilus G. Pinches and a description of it was given by Sir Henry Creswicke Rawlinson to the Royal Asiatic Society on 17 November 1879, followed by a publication in the society's journal the next year. Since then there have been a number of translations, the most recent of which was made by Dr Irving Finkel for the British Museum's 'Babylon' exhibition in 2008 and recently updated by him (see pp. 42–3). A new translation into Persian was at the same time made by Dr Shahrokh Razmjou (2010).

Since its arrival in the British Museum (fig. 13) the Cylinder was on display more or less continually, albeit in different locations, until it was first sent on loan in 1971. This happened

13 The Cyrus Cylinder on display in the Rahim Irvani Gallery of Ancient Iran at the British Museum in 2012.

in a curious way. In 1958, the idea came about in Tehran of celebrating the 2,500th anniversary of the foundation of the Persian empire by Cyrus the Great, and the celebrations were scheduled for 1961, that is 2,500 years after Cyrus captured Babylon in 539 BC. It is not clear now exactly with whom the idea originated, but it may have been Dr Shojaeddin Shafa, the Vice-Minister at the Imperial Court and adviser to Mohammad Reza Shah Pahlavi. At any rate, it was Shafa who proposed the idea to the Shah. Others who enthusiastically supported the proposal included André Malraux, the French Minister of Culture under General de Gaulle and David Ben-Gurion, Prime Minister of Israel 1948–54, who was an admirer of Cyrus because of his alleged favourable treatment of the Jews. Although the celebration was initially planned for 1961, it was postponed twice and did not actually take place until 1971. When it did happen it was an extravaganza on an unprecedented scale and made the Shah deeply unpopular with his own subjects and an object of ridicule worldwide. Six hundred VIP guests from around the world, including royal families and heads of state or their representatives, were invited to stay in a splendid tent city at Persepolis. The festivities lasted for four days (12–16 October 1971), and included a gala dinner with food supplied by Maxim's in Paris and a military parade with soldiers dressed in historical costumes representing Iran's glorious past. On the last day the Shah inaugurated the Shahyad Tower (now the Azadi Tower), a huge arch-like structure between Mehrabad Airport and Tehran city centre. At the base of this monument is a small museum where the Cyrus Cylinder was briefly on display between 16 and 19 October 1971. It was escorted to and from Tehran by Dr Richard Barnett, then Keeper of the Department of Western Asiatic Antiquities at the British Museum. There were demands for the Cylinder to be kept in Iran for a longer period, but Barnett was able to deflect these by explaining that the Cylinder had been promised for the British Museum's own exhibition on 'Royal Persia' that was scheduled to open on 29 October 1971. At the time the loan of the Cylinder to Iran was controversial, and not all parts of the British establishment, including the Foreign Office and the British royal family, had been properly briefed on the subject. This became clear through the research of Martin Bailey of the *Art Newspaper* into recently released government archives (*The Art Newspaper*, 1 September 2004).

The Cyrus Cylinder became the official symbol of the 2,500-year celebrations, and the logo shows the Cylinder surrounded by a garland of lotus flowers and surmounted by the imperial coat of arms of Iran. It appeared on a number of gold and silver medals (fig. 15), and also on gold and silver coins. The Cylinder is also featured on one of the four stamps issued by Iran on 12 October 1971 to commemorate the anniversary (fig. 14). Beneath the Cylinder is the inscription 'Proclamation de Cyrus le Grand'; this raises the question of when the Cylinder was originally called the first bill or declaration of human rights. In his book *Mission for my Country*, published in 1961, the Shah makes various complimentary references to Cyrus but says nothing specific about the Cylinder. In *The White Revolution of Iran*, however, published in 1967, he describes the Cylinder as 'the Charter of Liberty granted by Cyrus the Great', and in 1968, when opening a United Nations (UN) conference in Tehran on human rights, he referred to the Cylinder as 'the precursor to the modern Universal Declaration of Human Rights'. It seems likely, therefore, that the description of 'first bill of human rights' was first applied in the mid-1960s, but it could have been as early as 1958 when the idea of the 2,500-year celebration was first mooted. As we shall see, it is certainly a fanciful description, as it was never intended to be a document guaranteeing human rights and indeed the modern concept of human rights did not even exist at that time. However, the Cylinder has come to acquire a special resonance for Iranians, and it is now celebrated as a sort of national symbol. It is interesting that reverence for the Cylinder has outlasted the monarchy that promoted it in the first place, as attested by the popularity of the recent exhibition in Tehran (see below) and the fact that the Cylinder appeared on a sheet of stamps issued by the Islamic Republic to celebrate the Expo 2005 exhibition in Aichi, Japan (fig. 16). Beneath the image of the Cylinder is written 'The First World Charter of Human Rights'.

On 14 October 1971 the Shah's sister, Princess Ashraf, presented UN Secretary General U Thant with a replica of the Cylinder, and since then it has been on display in the UN Headquarters in New York, translated into all six official UN languages.

In 2005, the Cylinder was exhibited in the highly successful special exhibition at the British Museum, 'Forgotten Empire: the World of Ancient Persia', from 9 September 2005 until 8 January 2006 (Curtis and Tallis 2005). The sponsors of this exhibition, which attracted 154,200 visitors, included the Iran Heritage Foundation. After

14 (top left) First day cover with stamps issued on 12 October 1971 to commemorate the 2,500th anniversary of the founding of the Persian Empire.

15 (above) Gold medal issued to commemorate the 2,500th anniversary of the founding of the Persian Empire, showing on the reverse the Cyrus Cylinder.

16 (left) The Cyrus Cylinder shown on stamps issued by the Islamic Republic of Iran to celebrate the Expo 2005 exhibition in Japan.

London the exhibition, including the Cyrus Cylinder, travelled to Spain, where it was shown at the Fundación 'La Caixa' in Barcelona from 7 March to 11 June 2006. The Cyrus Cylinder also featured in the British Museum's special exhibition on 'Babylon: Myth and Reality', that was shown from 13 November to 15 March 2009 (Finkel and Seymour 2008). Previously, versions of this exhibition were presented in Paris and Berlin, but these did not include the Cyrus Cylinder.

Already in April 2003, when in Tehran to make preliminary enquiries about borrowing objects for the 'Forgotten Empire' exhibition, Neil MacGregor made the suggestion that the Trustees might be willing to countenance another loan of the Cylinder to Tehran, although it was never a condition of borrowing objects from Iran. Nevertheless, after receiving generous loans for the 'Forgotten Empire' and 'Shah 'Abbas' exhibitions (19 February–14 June 2009), the Trustees were keen to reciprocate by lending the Cylinder. Such a loan would also be in accordance with their policy of making the British Museum collection as widely accessible as possible, and give an Iranian audience an opportunity to see an iconic object that had great significance for them. There would also be the added benefit that at a time of tense political relations a loan would facilitate the continuation of a cultural dialogue.

Accordingly, it was arranged that the Cylinder should be loaned to Tehran for the period 16 January to 16 May 2010, when it would form the centrepiece of an exhibition devoted entirely to the Cylinder. However, the British Museum was obliged to reconsider the matter when there was an outbreak of violence in Iran, less than three weeks before the exhibition was due to open. This happened on ashura, the Shiite day of mourning that fell on 27 December. There had been simmering discontent in Iran since the previous June when the elections were disputed.

In the circumstances, given that the safety of the Cylinder (which was their prime responsibility) could not be assured, the Trustees reluctantly decided to postpone the loan. At the same time, by an extraordinary coincidence, two remarkable discoveries were made amongst the study collections of the Department of the Middle East. On 23 December 2009 and on 4 January 2010 two small fragments of a cuneiform tablet were discovered, by the late Professor Wilfred Lambert and Dr Irving Finkel respectively, which contained portions of a text duplicating that of the Cyrus Cylinder. The importance of these new discoveries and their implication for the significance of the Cyrus Cylinder was immediately realized, and it was decided that advantage should be taken of the postponement of the exhibition to organize an academic seminar which would give experts an opportunity to study and discuss the new fragments.

The seminar was arranged for 23–4 June 2010, and experts attended from all around the world, including the USA, Germany and China. It had been hoped that there would be some official Iranian involvement, but although some Iranian scholars attended the seminar there were no official representatives of the Iran Cultural Heritage, Handicrafts and Tourism Organization (ICHHTO).

During this period there were some tart exchanges between Iranian officials and the British Museum, with Iran protesting about breach of faith, but in truth the British Museum Trustees had unanimously agreed in the first place that the Cylinder could be loaned to Tehran and had never deviated from that position. The delay now was because of security concerns, not politics. Happily cordial relations were soon restored, and by 10 August 2010 the situation had stabilized sufficiently for Neil MacGregor to feel able to sign a contract in Tehran, agreeing to loan the Cylinder for the period 12 September 2010 to 12 January 2011.

In due course the Cylinder and the two new tablet fragments were taken to Tehran by a group

17 The opening ceremony of the Cyrus Cylinder exhibition in the National Museum of Iran, 12 September 2010.

18 (facing page) Photographers after the 'authentication' ceremony in the National Museum of Iran, 11 September 2010.

of four British Museum couriers comprising John Curtis, then Keeper of the Middle East Department, Ken Uprichard (then Head of Conservation), Dean Baylis, Senior Administrator in the Middle East Department and Vesta Sarkhosh Curtis, Curator of Middle East coins in the Department of Coins and Medals who also acted as translator. Neil MacGregor, Joanna Mackle, Director of Public Engagement, Karen Armstrong, historian of religions and British Museum Trustee and Birgit Brandt, British Academy, also came to Tehran for the opening ceremony on Sunday 12 September 2010 (fig. 17). This was preceded on the previous day by an 'authentication' ceremony in which nine Iranian experts were invited to participate. The purpose of this was to satisfy everybody that the real Cylinder was being put on show and not a copy. At the opening ceremony, Mrs Azadeh Ardakani, Director of the National Museum of Iran, Neil MacGregor, His Excellency Hamid Baghaei, the Vice-President of Iran and head of ICHHTO, His Excellency Esfandiar Rahim Mashaei, special adviser to the President of Iran and His Excellency Mahmoud Ahmadinejad, President of Iran, all gave speeches to an audience that included about thirty ambassadors and many other foreign and Iranian dignitaries. The Iranian speeches all stressed the great contribution made by Cyrus to Iranian history and culture and heralded the Cylinder as a civilizing influence and a proclamation of human rights. The ceremony took place in an auditorium where the stage was decorated in the style of Persepolis, with reconstructed friezes and relief decoration. Before and after the speeches there were musical performances, a nationalistic play featuring protectors of Iran, namely Cyrus the Great himself, Kaveh Ahangar, the blacksmith of the *Shahnama* (the Iranian national epic) who rescued Iran from the usurper Zahak, and a martyr (*basiji*) who protected the country in the Iraq–Iran war. There was also a film showing an Iranian soldier riding through Persian history in search of the Cyrus Cylinder, which he eventually finds in the National Museum.

The exhibition itself consisted of a single case containing the Cyrus Cylinder and the two tablet fragments centrally positioned in a large room on the upper floor of the National Museum (previously known as 'the treasure room'). Around the walls of the room were eleven panels with explanatory texts and illustrations supplied by the British Museum. Outside the exhibition hall, part of the upper floor of the Museum was decked out

with casts and photographs to resemble Persepolis, while the staircase to the upper floor was lined with photographs of figures climbing stairs, also at Persepolis. As the presentation of the Cylinder had been done in such a skilful and professional manner, and the security arrangements were entirely satisfactory, the Trustees had no qualms about agreeing to an extension of the loan until 17 April (to include the Nowruz holidays), subject to the signing of a new loan agreement and a memorandum of understanding relating entirely to cultural matters.

The exhibition was very popular, and although exact visitor numbers are not available it is thought that up to half a million people saw the exhibition; on one day alone in September 2010 (children's day on 10 Mehr) there were more than 10,000 visitors, but this was exceptional. At the closing ceremony of the exhibition on Saturday 16 April there were again speeches from Mrs Ardakani, Neil MacGregor, Mr Baghaei and Mr Mashaei, a musical performance and a recitation in the style of the Iranian epic poet Firdowsi of a newly written epic poem about Cyrus and the Cyrus Cylinder. On the same day, a brass plaque was unveiled in the porch of the National Museum commemorating the exhibition.

Lastly, it should be noted that contrary to the predictions of some sceptics before the exhibition, there was no attempt whatsoever by the Iranian government to impede the return of the Cylinder or to delay it in any way, and although at least one radical newspaper suggested at the start of the tour that the Cylinder should be impounded, this demand was soon dropped. The National Museum proved, as expected, to be a considerate and reliable partner, and the Iranian colleagues were a pleasure to work with.

Translation of the text by I.L. Finkel

1. *[When.......Mar]duk, king of the whole of heaven and earth, the.....who, in his..., lays waste his ...*
2. *[...] broad? in intelligence, ... who inspects (?) the [wor]ld quarters (regions)*
3. *[...] his [first]born (=Belshazzar), a low person, was put in charge of his country,*
4. *but [..] he set [a (...) counter]feit over them.*
5. *He ma[de] a counterfeit of Esagil, [and..............]... for Ur and the rest of the cult-cities.*
6. *Rites inappropriate to them, [impure] fo[od- offerings ....] disrespectful [...] were daily gabbled, and, as an insult,*
7. *he brought the daily offerings to a halt; he inter[fered with the rites and] instituted [.......] within the sanctuaries. In his mind, reverential fear of Marduk, king of the gods, came to an end.*
8. *He did yet more evil to his city every day; ... his [people...................], he brought ruin on them all by a yoke without relief.*
9. *Enlil-of-the-gods became extremely angry at their complaints, and [...] their territory. The gods who lived within them left their shrines,*
10. *angry that he had made (them) enter into Shuanna (Babylon). Ex[alted Marduk, Enlil-of-the-Go]ds, relented. He changed his mind about all the settlements whose sanctuaries were in ruins,*
11. *and the population of the land of Sumer and Akkad who had become like corpses, and took pity on them. He inspected and checked all the countries,*
12. *seeking for the upright king of his choice. He took the hand of Cyrus, king of the city of Anshan, and called him by his name, proclaiming him aloud for the kingship over all of everything.*
13. *He made the land of Guti and all the Median troops prostrate themselves at his feet, while he shepherded in justice and righteousness the black-headed people*
14. *whom he had put under his care. Marduk, the great lord, who nurtures his people, saw with pleasure his fine deeds and true heart,*
15. *and ordered that he should go to Babylon. He had him take the road to Tintir (Babylon), and, like a friend and companion, he walked at his side.*
16. *His vast troops whose number, like the water in a river, could not be counted, were marching fully-armed at his side.*
17. *He had him enter without fighting or battle right into Shuanna; he saved his city Babylon from hardship. He handed over to him Nabonidus, the king who did not fear him.*
18. *All the people of Tintir, of all Sumer and Akkad, nobles and governors, bowed down before him and kissed his feet, rejoicing over his kingship and their faces shone.*
19. *The lord through whose help all were rescued from death and who saved them all from distress and hardship, they blessed him sweetly and praised his name.*
20. *I am Cyrus, king of the universe, the great king, the powerful king, king of Babylon, king of Sumer and Akkad, king of the four quarters of the world,*
21. *son of Cambyses, the great king, king of the city of Anshan, grandson of Cyrus, the great king, ki[ng of the ci]ty of Anshan, descendant of Teispes, the great king, king of the city of Anshan,*
22. *the perpetual seed of kingship, whose reign Bel (Marduk)and Nabu love, and with whose kingship, to their joy, they concern themselves. When I went as harbinger of peace i[nt]o Babylon*
23. *I founded my sovereign residence within the palace amid celebration and rejoicing.*

Marduk, the great lord, bestowed on me as my destiny the great magnanimity of one who loves Babylon, and I every day sought him out in awe.

24. *My vast troops were marching peaceably in Babylon, and the whole of [Sumer] and Akkad had nothing to fear.*
25. *I sought the safety of the city of Babylon and all its sanctuaries. As for the population of Babylon [..., w]ho as if without div[ine intention] had endured a yoke not decreed for them,*
26. *I soothed their weariness; I freed them from their bonds(?). Marduk, the great lord, rejoiced at [my good] deeds,*
27. *and he pronounced a sweet blessing over me, Cyrus, the king who fears him, and over Cambyses, the son [my] issue, [and over] my all my troops,*
28. *that we might live happily in his presence, in well-being. At his exalted command, all kings who sit on thrones,*
29. *from every quarter, from the Upper Sea to the Lower Sea, those who inhabit [remote distric]ts (and) the kings of the land of Amurru who live in tents, all of them,*
30. *brought their weighty tribute into Shuanna, and kissed my feet. From [Shuanna] I sent back to their places to the city of Ashur and Susa,*
31. *Akkad, the land of Eshnunna, the city of Zamban, the city of Meturnu, Der, as far as the border of the land of Guti – the sanctuaries across the River Tigris – whose shrines had earlier become dilapidated,*
32. *the gods who lived therein, and made permanent sanctuaries for them. I collected together all of their people and returned them to their settlements,*
33. *and the gods of the land of Sumer and Akkad which Nabonidus – to the fury of the lord of the gods – had brought into Shuanna, at the command of Marduk, the great lord,*
34. *I returned them unharmed to their cells, in the sanctuaries that make them happy. May all the gods that I returned to their sanctuaries,*
35. *every day before Bel and Nabu, ask for a long life for me, and mention my good deeds, and say to Marduk, my lord, this: 'Cyrus, the king who fears you, and Cambyses his son,*
36. *may they be the provisioners of our shrines until distant (?) days, and the population of Babylon call blessings on my kingship. I have enabled all the lands to live in peace.*
37. *Every day I increased by [... ge]ese, two ducks and ten pigeons the [former offerings] of geese, ducks and pigeons.*
38. *I strove to strengthen the defences of the wall Imgur-Enlil, the great wall of Babylon,*
39. *and [I completed] the quay of baked brick on the bank of the moat which an earlier king had bu[ilt but not com]pleted its work.*
40. *[I ...... which did not surround the city] outside, which no earlier king had built, his workforce, the levee [from his land, in/int]o Shuanna.*
41. *[..with bitum]en and baked brick I built anew, and [completed] its [work].*
42. *[...] great [doors of cedarwood] with bronze cladding,*
43. *[and I installed] all their doors, threshold slabs and door fittings with copper parts. [.........................] I saw within it an inscription of Ashurbanipal, a king who preceded me;*
44. *[...] in its place. May Marduk, the great lord, present to me as a gift a long life and the fullness of age,*
45. *[a secure throne and an enduring rei]gn, [and may I ...... in] your heart forever.*

[Written and check]ed [from a...]; (this) tablet (is) of Qishti-Marduk, son of [...].

(Underlined text indicates information from new tablet fragments)

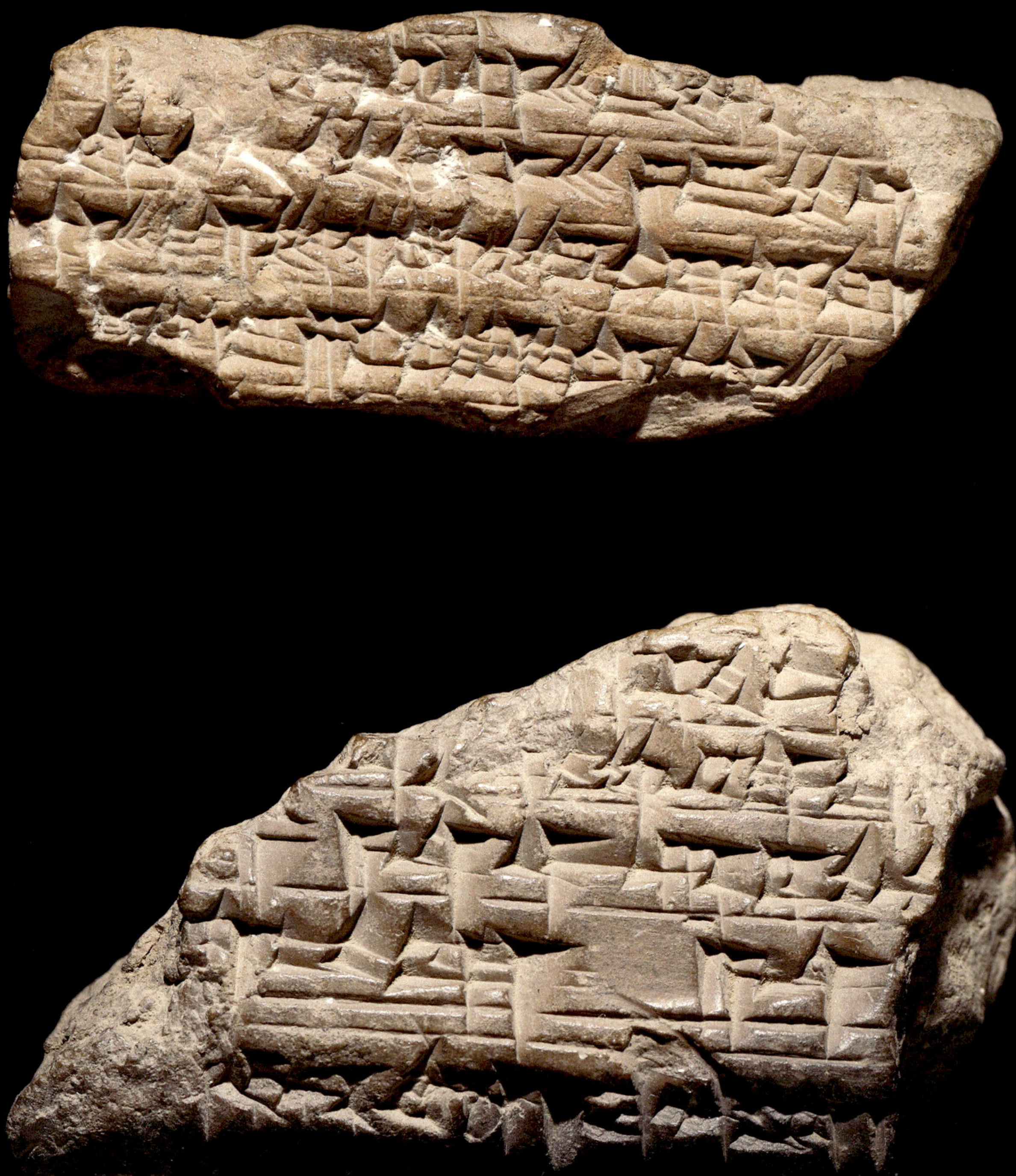

2
3

Fragments of cuneiform tablet

539–538 BC (?), Achaemenid period
Excavated in Babylon, Dilbat or Borsippa in 1880–1
Unbaked clay

2 1.7 x 4.3 cm, thickness 1.9 cm
BM 47176 (1881,0830.698)

3 2.7 x 4.1 cm, thickness 2.0 cm
BM 47134 (1881,0830.656)

The two fragments belong to a single large cuneiform tablet and were sent to the British Museum with a mixed collection of inscribed material obtained in the excavations of Hormuzd Rassam at Babylon, Dailem (ancient Dilbat, about 30 km south of Babylon) and Ibrahim al-Khalil (next to Birs Nimrud, ancient Borsippa, about 25 km south-west of Babylon) in 1880–1. Although any of these three sites is a possible provenance for the two tablet fragments, Babylon is perhaps the most likely. The fragment cat. no. 2 was identified as belonging to a tablet replicating part of the Cyrus Cylinder by the late Professor W.G. Lambert on 23 December 2009, while the fragment cat. no. 3 was identified by Dr Irving Finkel on 4 January 2010. Alerted to the discovery of Professor Lambert on 4 January, Dr Finkel immediately searched for other fragments in the collection registered in the British Museum under the number 1881-8-30, and discovered the second fragment. There is no doubt that the two fragments belong to the same distinctive cuneiform tablet, made of good quality clay; it would originally have been quite large, and is definitely a tablet rather than a barrel cylinder. Both fragments are said by Dr Finkel to be written in an accomplished and professional scribal hand that is readily identifiable; in addition, every line of the tablet is ruled, and the last line is finished off with a double ruling. The fragment cat. no. 2 is one-sided, and not only duplicates lines 34–7 of the Cyrus Cylinder inscription, but adds some important new information that was missing. The fragment cat. no. 3 comes from the top edge of the tablet and has new material both from the beginning (lines 1–2) and the end (lines 44–5) of the Cylinder inscription, which are the main areas of loss in the Cylinder. This piece includes the name of the scribe who wrote out or copied the tablet; he gives his name in the one-line colophon (scribal note) at the end of the tablet as Qishti-Marduk (son of Marduk), or possibly Iqish-Marduk, son of a man whose name is missing. In Dr Finkel's translation of the Cylinder inscription (pp. 42–3), the snippets of information added by the new fragments, with two further references to Marduk, are underlined.

It is clear that the two fragments cat. nos 2–3 belonged to a large cuneiform tablet that replicated the text inscribed on the Cyrus Cylinder. The discovery of these fragments was of great significance because they show that the Cylinder was not a unique document, and that copies of it existed certainly on clay tablets and perhaps in other mediums, which is discussed further below.

4

Brick with inscription of Cyrus

539–530 BC, Achaemenid period
Excavated in Ur, Iraq, 1922–3 season
Baked clay

32.5 x 32.0 cm, thickness 6.0 cm
BM 118362 (1923,1110, 221)

This brick is stamped with a six-line inscription in Babylonian which translates as: 'Cyrus, king of the world, king of Anshan, son of Cambyses, king of Anshan. The great gods delivered all the lands into my hand, and I made this land to dwell in peace.'

It was excavated at Ur (fig. 19) during the British Museum–University of Pennsylvania excavations directed by Sir Leonard Woolley. The brick was found with other similar examples in a gateway in the north-east wall of the inner enclosure (temenos). The bricks had been used to build a box against the south-east door-jamb for the pivot-stone on which the gate turned. Because of the inscribed bricks, Woolley called this the 'Cyrus Gate'. Another inscribed brick of Cyrus in the British Museum collection was found at Warka, also in Mesopotamia (Walker 1981, no. 116). The inscription reads 'Cyrus, beloved of Esagil and Ezida, son of Cambyses, mighty king am I.'

19 View of the restored ziggurat (temple tower) at Ur in southern Iraq.

Commentary on cat. nos 2–4

What is the significance of the Cyrus Cylinder? As we have seen, it was adopted as the symbol of the 2,500th anniversary of the foundation of the Persian empire in 1971, and was vigorously promoted as the first Declaration of Human Rights. The Cylinder was regarded then, as it is still regarded by many, as a document confirming the impression of Cyrus given by the Bible and some classical authors as a champion of liberal and humanitarian values and a defender of human rights. The passage in the Cylinder which has given rise to these assumptions is lines 31–5, which tells us that Cyrus returned to various places statues of gods that had presumably been brought to Shuanna (Babylon) by the previous Babylonian kings. The places mentioned are 'the city of Ashur and Susa, Akkad, the land of Eshnunna, the city of Zamban, the city of Meturnu, Der, as far as the border of the land of Guti [and] the sanctuaries across the River Tigris'. The shrines to which these statues were returned were also restored. And then, and this is particularly significant, he says, 'I collected together all of their people and returned them to their settlements.' Lastly, we are told that he also returned to their sanctuaries the god statues of the land of Sumer and Akkad that had been brought to Babylon by Nabonidus.

Advocates of the special significance of the Cylinder argue that by returning god statues and restoring shrines, Cyrus was condoning if not actually promoting the worship of various gods and the practice of various religions. Further, by returning people 'to their settlements' he is effectively repatriating people who had been deported by the Babylonian kings. In both these areas, supporters claim, Cyrus is departing from previous practice and is doing something new, but is this true?

Sceptics argue that the Cyrus Cylinder is a foundation inscription of typical Babylonian type and does not depart from the traditional model, either in terms of its shape or its content. They compare the Cyrus Cylinder with barrel cylinders of the preceding Babylonian kings and argue that Cyrus is merely following standard Babylonian practice. Close parallels are also to be found with the foundation inscriptions of Assyrian kings, particularly Esarhaddon and Ashurbanipal. There are certainly similarities. Thus, in his clay prisms recording the restoration of Babylon, Esarhaddon says that he has been instructed to do these good works by Marduk, and he describes the building works. In one text (Babylon Prism C) he says: 'He [the god Marduk] ordered me to complete the cult centres, to renovate the shrines, [and] to organize well the rites of Esagil, the palace of the gods', and further on: 'I returned the plundered gods of the lands (fr)om Assyria and the land Elam to their proper) place(s), and I set up proper procedures in all of the cult centres.' It appears, then, that Cyrus may be following precedent when he sent statues of gods back to the shrines from which they had been seized, as Esarhaddon also claimed to have sent god statues from Babylon back to Assyria and Elam. However, the scale of the operation under Cyrus may have been much greater, given that he mentions more places than Esarhaddon. Also, it is reasonable to conclude that although the places referred to are restricted to Babylonia, Assyria and Iran, they may also have included places to the west which were not mentioned because Cyrus was writing for a Babylonian audience. More remarkable than the list of places to which god statues were returned, however, is the statement that people were returned to their settlements, which does not seem to be part of the usual rubric of Assyrian or Babylonian inscriptions. Therefore, we may tentatively conclude that the Cylinder does show some evidence of a departure from the standard foundation inscription. That the Cylinder is written in Babylonian style and using Babylonian phraseology is irrelevant, as we know that it was written by a Babylonian scribe in, of course, the Babylonian language.

The biblical references to Cyrus certainly support the view that his policies (whatever might have motivated them) found favour with at least some of his contemporaries. For example, we read in the Book of Isaiah that God says of Cyrus, 'He is my shepherd and will accomplish all that I please; he will say of Jerusalem, Let it be rebuilt and of the temple, Let its foundations be laid' (Isaiah 44, v. 28). And then, 'This is what the Lord says to his anointed [literally his Messiah], to Cyrus…I will go before you…so that you may know that I am the Lord, the God of Israel…and (I will) bestow on you a title of honour, though you do not acknowledge me', and 'I will strengthen you, though you have not acknowledged me' (Isaiah 45, vv. 1–5).

At the end of 2 Chronicles we are told that because of the wickedness of King Zedekiah the Lord allowed Nebuchadnezzar, King of Babylon to attack Jerusalem; he slaughtered many of the inhabitants, carried off to Babylon the temple treasures, burned the temple, and deported to Babylon the inhabitants who had survived the massacre. Then:

> In the first year of Cyrus king of Persia, in order to fulfil the word of the Lord spoken by Jeremiah, the Lord moved the heart of Cyrus king of Persia to make a proclamation throughout his realm and put it in writing: This is what Cyrus king of Persia says: "The Lord, the God of heaven, has given me all the kingdoms of the earth and he has appointed me to build a temple for him at Jerusalem in Judah. Anyone of his people among you – may the Lord his God be with you, and let him go up." (2 Chronicles 36, vv. 22–3)

The story is then taken up in the first Book of Ezra, which repeats the last two verses of 2 Chronicles, and goes on to describe how Cyrus decreed that all Jews should return to Jerusalem to help in the rebuilding of the temple, both physically and financially. He also returns to Jerusalem all the temple treasures (5,400 articles in gold and silver altogether) that Nebuchadnezzar had removed to Babylon. There follows a list of the returning exiles, who are said to number 42,360 with 7,337 servants and 200 singers.

According to the Bible, then, Cyrus liberated the Jews from their Babylonian exile and sent them back to Jerusalem to rebuild the temple. This is presented as a momentous event, something that is quite out of the ordinary, perhaps unprecedented. Of course the Cyrus Cylinder does not mention Judah, or rebuilding the temple in Jerusalem, but it does refer to the restoration of shrines and the repatriation of deported peoples. It is therefore reasonable to connect the biblical story with the account in the Cylinder.

We also have the testimony of the classical authors; Herodotus greatly admired Cyrus, and Cyrus is made the subject of a novel, or political romance, by Xenophon in his *Cyropaedia*. The book is based on the life of Cyrus, although it is partly fictional, and presents him as an ideal ruler. It is a measure of the impact that the book has had that *Cyropaedia* is said to have been required reading, alongside Machiavelli's *The Prince*, for many of the Founding Fathers of the United States of America. Thomas Jefferson is reputed to have had two copies.

Given the biblical and classical accounts of the life of Cyrus, it seems clear that we are entitled to view the Cyrus Cylinder as more than a standard Babylonian building inscription, although we must certainly stop short of regarding it as some kind of statement about human rights. In assessing the significance of the Cylinder, however, the discovery of the two new fragments of tablet (cat. nos 2–3) is of great significance. These show that the Cylinder was not a unique document and that other copies existed, certainly in the forms of clay tablets but possibly other mediums as well. Of course it could be argued that the tablet was a draft or prototype for the Cylinder inscription, or even some kind of 'file copy', but this seems unlikely. This therefore raises the possibility that the Cylinder contained (perhaps only in part) the text of some kind of proclamation.

There are precedents for Achaemenid kings issuing proclamations. Thus, we know that versions of Darius' great inscription at Bisitun were circulated around the empire. Darius himself says in the Old Persian version of the Bisitun inscription:

> Saith Darius the King: by the favour of Ahuramazda this is the inscription which I

> made. Besides, it was in Aryan, and on clay tablets and on parchment it was composed. Besides, a sculptured figure of myself I made. Besides, I made my lineage. And it was inscribed and was read off before me. Afterwards this inscription I sent off everywhere amongst the provinces. The people unitedly worked upon it (Kent, p. 132, S 70).

We also have the evidence of the stele found at Babylon (see pp. 72–3) which, although in fragments, apparently reproduces on the reverse the Babylonian version (or part of it) of the Bisitun inscription. There is even an Aramaic version of the Bisitun inscription found at Elephantine in Egypt. It is by no means implausible, then, that Cyrus issued a proclamation of the same kind. Indeed, there is a hint in the biblical record of such a proclamation. According to the Book of Ezra, there had been little progress with the rebuilding of the temple by the reign of Darius (apparently for reasons of local politics) and the builders were asked to justify the project. A letter was sent to Darius claiming that Cyrus had issued a decree ordering the temple to be rebuilt. Darius ordered a search to be made and a scroll was found not in Babylon as expected but in the citadel of Ecbatana, recording that Cyrus issued a decree ordering that the temple should be rebuilt and paid for by the royal treasury. As a result, Darius issued a new decree ordering that the temple should be rebuilt (Ezra 5, vv. 13–17; 6, v. 12). This story should probably not be taken at face value, but it does perhaps testify to the issuing of decrees and the storage of them.

It is sometimes claimed that Cyrus was especially tolerant of the Jews because he recognized in them a belief in monotheism that was in line with his own religious faith. Before considering the validity of these claims, what do we know of Cyrus' own religious beliefs? As we shall see when discussing the gold plaque (cat. no. 7), Darius and his successors pay tribute to Ahuramazda and should most properly be described as worshippers of Ahuramazda, or Mazda worshippers. We do not know if they were Zoroastrians in the sense that they were aware of and followed the teachings of the prophet Zoroaster. At the same time, they were happy to support and at least pay lip service to other religions, even in the vicinity of Persepolis. For Cyrus, we are starved of information. He left no monumental inscriptions in Old Persian extolling Ahuramazda, so we cannot be sure that he was a Mazda worshipper. However, given his Iranian background, it is highly unlikely that he was not, and authorities such as Mary Boyce have argued strongly that he was a Zoroastrian. They cite the existence of what seem to be fire altars at Pasargadae, the curious Zendan-i Sulaiman tower

20 The Zendan-i Sulaiman (prison of Solomon) at Pasargadae. The purpose of this building is unknown, but it may have had a religious function.

(fig. 20) and the nature of his own tomb (fig. 21). We also have the possible testimony of Xenophon, that there were magi (Zoroastrian priests) at his court (*Cyropaedia* VIII.i.23), although Xenophon's account is more fictional than historical. If Cyrus was indeed then a Mazda worshipper, or even a Zoroastrian, how can we reconcile this with what else we know about him? In the Cylinder itself, we see that Cyrus acts in accordance with the wishes of the Babylonian god Marduk, whom he calls 'my lord'. He also asks that the gods whom he returns to their shrines should intercede with Marduk and Nabu (the son of Marduk and the Babylonian god of wisdom and writing) on his behalf. In other contexts, Cyrus supports different gods. He undertook restoration work at Warka, where there was a sanctuary of Ishtar. A cylinder found at Ur recording the restoration of the sanctuary of Sin, the Babylonian moon god, possibly (but not certainly) dates from the time of Cyrus. The explanation for this is that it was customary at that time for kings to respect other people's gods, and even to recognize that they had authority in their own countries. For this reason it was obligatory for Cyrus to pay respect to Marduk when he entered Babylon, but this does not mean that he revered Marduk above all other gods. We can see the same situation in the Bible. On the one hand, Cyrus says, 'The Lord, the God of heaven, has given me all the kingdoms of the earth' (2 Chronicles 36, v. 23), but on the other hand the Lord God of Israel says He will 'bestow on you a title of honour, though you do not acknowledge me', and 'I will strengthen you, though you have not acknowledged me' (Isaiah 45, vv. 4–5). This is entirely in accord with prevailing contemporary views: gods had a national identity, with authority over their own people, and were not perceived as the only gods who existed. Thus in the Books of Ezra and Nehemiah, Yahweh is presented as

21 The Tomb of Cyrus at Pasargadae, 6th century BC.

the god of the Israelites, not as the only god who prevails over the whole world.

What implications does this have for Cyrus' statements in the Cylinder? The first point to recognize is that there was no attempt in the Achaemenid period, nor had there been in the preceding Assyrian and Babylonian periods, to impose a religion on conquered people. Indeed, the concept of a state religion that needed to be carried abroad did not exist at this time. Thus, we should be cautious about making extravagant claims about Cyrus following a policy of religious toleration. Clearly he was libertarian and enlightened in returning god statues to sanctuaries and peoples to their homelands, but there had been no attempt to suppress the religions that he allowed to flourish. In short, we cannot conclude that Cyrus was sympathetic towards the Jews because they both believed in monotheistic religions.

Chapter III

The Main Cities of the Persian Empire

It is clear from the classical sources if not from the Achaemenid texts themselves that the Persian kings and their court rotated annually around the major centres of Susa, Hamadan and Babylon. In addition to these places, we know that Pasargadae was an early foundation of Cyrus the Great and Persepolis was the jewel in the crown on the Iranian plateau, although hardly known, it seems, to the classical authors. Of the Persian kings, Darius was clearly the most energetic builder with a programme that matched his territorial ambitions. He launched at least two grandiose building projects, notably at Persepolis and Susa. Of the two schemes, Persepolis, which was continued by Xerxes, was the more ambitious, but probably the two centres were intended for different purposes which are not entirely clear to us. In any case, they served different constituencies: Persepolis was on the Iranian plateau in the heart of the modern province of Fars, whereas Susa was in the lowlands, facing Mesopotamia.

Pasargadae

The earliest of the major Persian centres is Pasargadae which Cyrus founded, probably soon after his conquest of Lydia. It is on the Iranian plateau some 90 km north-east of Shiraz. The surviving ruins consist of a small number of buildings widely spaced out across the plain.

The gateway to the complex (Gate R) has columns and entrances apparently flanked by Assyrian-style winged bulls. These no longer survive, but a stone relief on one of the door-jambs is still in position at the site although sadly less complete than it was in the early nineteenth century. It shows a four-winged genie (fig. 22) wearing an Egyptian crown which had a trilingual inscription above (now missing) in Old Persian, Elamite and Babylonian, probably added in the time of Darius, that read: 'I, Cyrus, the king, an Achaemenian.'

22 (facing page) Watercolour by Sir Robert Ker Porter in 1818 showing a stone relief with a winged genie in the gatehouse at Pasargadae. The top of the relief with a trilingual cuneiform inscription is now missing.

23 The stone columns of Palace P at Pasargadae, 6th century BC.

Then there are two small palaces and two pavilions. Palace S (the 'audience palace') has a central hall with eight columns surrounded by columned porticoes on all four sides and two corner towers. There is a combination of black and white stone in this palace, producing a pleasing artistic effect. Stone capitals for the columns apparently included lion, bull and horse figures. Originally there were eight stone antae or corner pillars flanking the four porticoes with trilingual inscriptions recording: 'I, Cyrus, the king, an Achaemenian.' These inscriptions are also thought to have been added by Darius. The four entrances to the central hall were lined with carved stone reliefs of which only the bottom parts survive, now in poor condition. The figures are in Assyrian style and include a man in a fish-cloak, a bull-man, a genie with eagle's talons and a human figure. Palace P (the 'residential palace') (fig. 23), about 300 m north of Palace S, also had corner pillars with inscriptions of Cyrus (fig. 24) and made use of black and white stone, but here the ground-plan is quite different to that of Palace S. There is a central rectangular hall with thirty columns with rooms at either end of it. There are two columned porticoes on either side of the central hall, but they are of different lengths. The stone reliefs that decorated the doorways connecting the central hall with the porticoes show the king followed by an attendant and are in Persian rather than Assyrian style. They were probably added in the time of Darius. An

24 Pillar in Palace P at Pasargadae with inscriptions mentioning Cyrus in Old Persian, Elamite and Babylonian cuneiform. These inscriptions were probably added in the time of Darius. 6th century BC.

inscription on the robe of the king reads: 'Cyrus, the *great* king, an Achaemenian.' Some fragments of painted plaster were found in this palace.

Between the two palaces there are two small structures that have been interpreted as pavilions. They have columned rooms in the middle with porticoes on all four sides. Beneath one of the pavilions a hoard of jewellery was found, buried in a pottery jar. It contained more than 1,000 items including ibex-headed bracelets and gold earrings (see figs 84 and 85). The existence of these pavilions, plus extensive evidence for stone-lined water channels, has led to suggestions that the central part of the site was turned over to formal gardens (fig. 25). Other features that we should mention at Pasargadae include the Zendan-i Sulaiman (prison of Solomon), an enigmatic stone tower with blind windows that is paralleled by a similar structure at Naqsh-i Rustam (see below), known as the Kabah-i Zardusht. The purpose of these structures is quite unknown but could have been religious. Then there is the Tall-i Takht, a gigantic stone platform partly carved out of the side of a natural hill that may have been intended for a palace that was never built. In the so-called sacred precinct to the north-west of the main site are two limestone plinths that have been identified as altars.

Cyrus was eventually killed in 530 BC whilst campaigning against the Massagetae on his north-east frontier, but his body was brought back to Pasargadae and buried in a massive stone-built tomb. This Tomb of Cyrus has a gabled roof and stands on a stepped platform built from large blocks of stone (fig. 21).

25 (below) Plan of Pasargadae showing the palaces, gardens and water courses, made before a recent geomagnetic survey which indicates that some revisions are necessary to the plan of the gardens.

26 (below right) Plan of Susa showing the main Achaemenid period buildings.

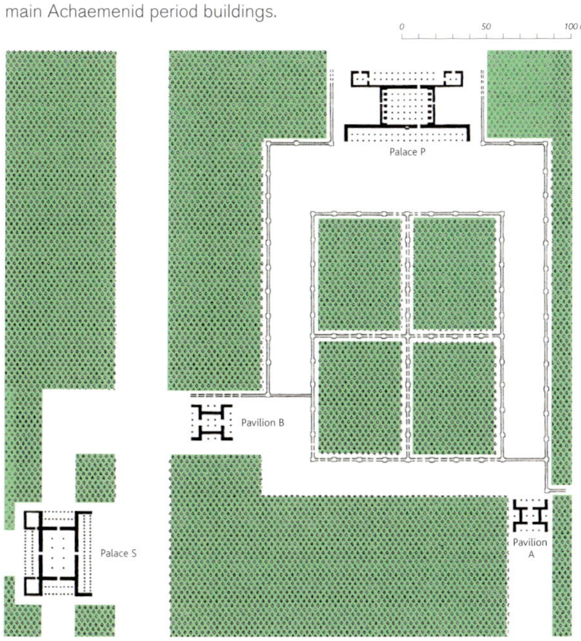

Susa

It is clear from Achaemenid royal inscriptions, the classical authors and the Bible that Susa was an important capital city in the Achaemenid period. The site is about 100 km north of Ahvaz, in the lowland part of Iran to the north of the head of the Persian Gulf. It consists of three gigantic mounds, occupying an area of about 1 square kilometre (fig. 26), known as the Apadana mound, the Acropolis mound (rising 36 m above the plain) and the Ville Royale (royal town) mound. Between about 3000 BC and the beginning of the

Because of the apparent lack of buildings at Pasargadae archaeologists have puzzled over its interpretation, but recent resistivity surveys have shown the existence of extensive residential quarters, albeit not in the central part of the site which was given over to a garden. After Cyrus, Darius was evidently active at Pasargadae (note the inscriptions and the reliefs in Palace P, and the platform may even have been levelled as a palace for him) and it is likely that Pasargadae continued in use, perhaps largely as a ceremonial and religious centre, until the end of the Achaemenid period. Plutarch records that the investiture of the Persian kings took place there.

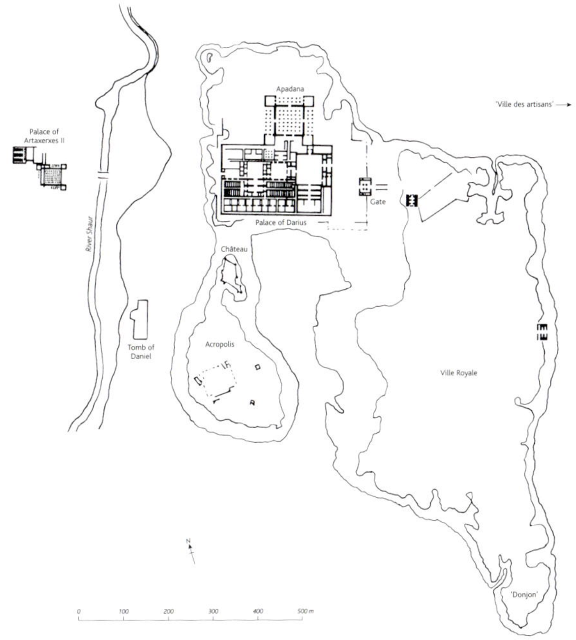

27 (below left) A double bull column capital on the site of Darius' Palace at Susa.

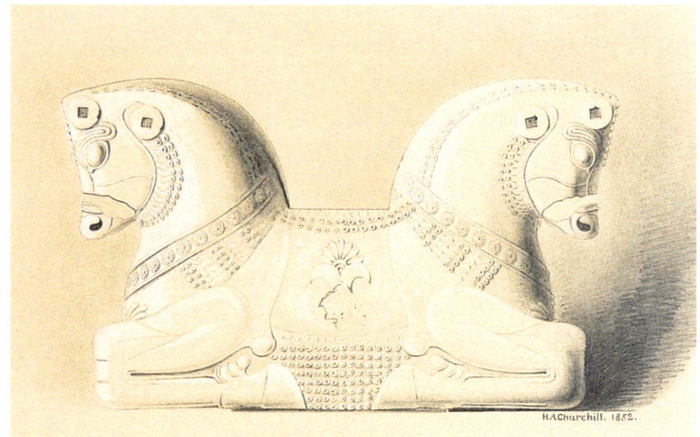

28 (below right) Double bull column capital from the Palace of Darius at Susa, found during the excavations of W.K. Loftus in 1850–2 and drawn by H.A. Churchill.

29 (bottom left) Column base from the Palace of Darius at Susa with cuneiform inscriptions of Xerxes (486–465 BC) in Old Persian, Elamite and Babylonian. Musée du Louvre (Sb 131, h. 39 cm, diam. 55 cm).

Achaemenid period, Susa was an important centre of Elamite civilization.

Darius is thought to have begun his building programme at Susa in about 519 BC, shortly before or perhaps even at the same time as Persepolis. On the Apadana mound he constructed an enormous palace consisting of a columned hall in the Iranian style adjoining an extensive mud brick building that owed more to the Mesopotamian tradition. In this way there was a neat fusion of highland and lowland, new and old. In the square central part of the columned hall were thirty-six stone columns, with columned porticoes on three sides and corner-towers. The fluted stone columns supported bull-shaped capitals (figs 27 and 28). Four of the column bases (fig. 29) in the central hall had inscriptions recording that the palace was originally built by Darius, had burnt down in the time of Artaxerxes I, and was rebuilt by Artaxerxes II.

While this hypostyle hall is likely to have been used for formal receptions and affairs of state, the adjoining palace was apparently residential and administrative. It is an enormous building, measuring 246 m x 155 m, and constructed from mud brick. Essentially, the rooms are arranged around three large courtyards, very much in the Assyrian and Babylonian style. On the south side of the west court there are two large rooms that have long been interpreted as the royal apartments. Although built in mud brick the Residence was not without decoration. There were red floors in the private parts of the building,

30 (left) Glazed brick panel from Susa showing a guard in Persian costume with a spear, bow and quiver. This figure was part of a row of guards, probably the 'Immortals' who formed the king's personal bodyguard. British Museum on loan from Musée du Louvre, 6th–5th century BC (BM 132525, 198 x 70 cm).

31 (below) Large clay tablet with foundation inscription of Darius (522–486 BC) written in Old Persian cuneiform. It describes the construction of his palace at Susa and records how he brought workmen and materials from different parts of the empire. Musée du Louvre (Sb 2789, 22.5 x 26.6 cm, thickness 2.5 cm).

as well as glazed brick decoration principally in the courtyards. Many of these bricks belong to the friezes of archers (fig. 30), sometimes thought to be the 'Immortals' who formed the king's personal bodyguard, and friezes of lions. In addition there are panels showing pairs of winged human-headed lions seated beneath a winged disc, and composite monsters such as winged bulls and griffins. In his Foundation Charter (fig. 31), Darius describes in detail how the foundations of the palace were dug, and he relates how materials and workmen were brought from different parts of the empire. Cedar wood came from the Lebanon, yaka-timber from Gandara and Carmania, gold from Sardis and Bactria, lapis lazuli and carnelian from Sogdiana, turquoise from Chorasmia,

32 Statue of Darius (522–486 BC) carved in Egypt and brought to Susa in antiquity. It has inscriptions in Old Persian, Elamite and Babylonian cuneiform and in Egyptian hieroglyphs. National Museum of Iran (4112, h. 2.66m).

33 (facing page, left) Part of an alabaster vase (alabastron) found by W.K. Loftus at Susa with a trilingual cuneiform inscription in Old Persian, Elamite and Babylonian recording 'Xerxes great king'. British Museum, 5th century BC (BM 91459, h. 16 cm).

34 (facing page, right) The Tomb of Daniel at Susa with its distinctive conical roof. The building dates from the medieval period.

silver and ebony from Egypt, ivory from Ethiopia, Sind and Arachosia, and stone columns from the village of Abiradu in Elam. As regards to workmen, he says that the stonemasons were Ionians and Sardians, the goldsmiths were Medes and Egyptians, the carpenters were Sardians and Egyptians, the men who made the baked brick were Babylonians, and 'the men who adorned the wall' were Medes and Egyptians.

Access to the palace was through the Gate of Darius on the eastern edge of the Apadana mound. In the middle of this building was a small columned hall, and an inscription by Xerxes recording that he had completed the building begun by his father Darius. It was in this gateway that a statue of Darius was found in 1972. Although the head is missing, it is a remarkable work of art that now occupies pride of place in the National Museum in Tehran (fig. 32). Darius is shown wearing a Persian robe, with a dorsal pillar (an Egyptian device) at his back. He stands on a rectangular base which has on its two long sides twenty-four 'fortress cartouches' with names in Egyptian hieroglyphs of the peoples belonging to the Persian empire, and above each cartouche is a kneeling figure with arms upraised dressed in the traditional costume of his country. On the short sides of the base are Egyptian fertility figures. The style of the statue, the inscriptions in Elamite, Old Persian, Babylonian and Egyptian (which record that 'the Persian man has conquered Egypt'), and the green schist stone that comes from Wadi Hammamat in Egypt, all show that the statue was made in Egypt, apparently to commemorate the inauguration of Darius' canal that connected the Nile with the Red Sea. It may originally have been set up at Pithom (Tell el-Maskhuta) to the east of the Nile Delta. Why and when it was brought to Susa is unknown.

The Acropolis mound was surrounded by a substantial Achaemenid wall leading to suggestions that the Treasury referred to by the Greek authors and looted by Alexander in 331 BC may have been here, but no trace of such a building has been found. There was, however, a burial in a bronze coffin with a rich collection of gold jewellery including a torque, a pair of lion-

headed bracelets, a pair of earrings and a pair of roundels (figs 83 and 84). In the north part of the Acropolis mound was found a large collection of fragments of alabaster vases (fig. 33) inscribed with the name of Xerxes in Old Persian, Elamite, Babylonian and Egyptian.

On the west bank of the River Shaur that flows through the site, and nearly 500 m to the west of the columned hall of Darius, is another cluster of Achaemenid period buildings only a few metres above the level of the plain that has come to be known as the Shaur Palace. The best preserved of these buildings is a columned hall about one third the size of that of Darius. Fragments of inscribed column base found in the Shaur Palace complex show that it was built by Artaxerxes II. The site may have been chosen for its idyllic location close to the river.

The Achaemenid period at Susa is also evidenced in the Bible, mainly through the events described in the Book of Esther. According to this tradition, Esther, a young Jewish girl who became a concubine of King Xerxes, was able to prevent a threatened massacre of Jews, a deliverance that is still remembered in the Jewish festival of Purim. It was also at Susa that Daniel had his dream about the ram and the goat, and Nehemiah was at Susa when he received the news that the walls and gates of Jerusalem had fallen into disrepair. The tomb of the prophet Daniel that is nowadays a notable landmark in Susa probably dates from the medieval period (fig. 34).

35 The 'Gate of All Nations' at Persepolis with pairs of winged human-headed bulls at either end and four columns between. 5th century BC.

Persepolis

The great city of Persepolis is certainly the best preserved and most impressive of the Achaemenid capitals, and today is justly famous throughout the world. Yet for some inexplicable reason it was hardly known to the classical authors. It is situated on the Iranian plateau, about 1770 m above sea level, nearly 50 km north-east of Shiraz. The city was founded on a platform of natural rock, levelled off by the Achaemenid builders, at the western foot of the Kuh-i Rahmat (Mountain of Mercy). This platform is about the same length as the acropolis at Athens (*c.* 455 m) but four to five times as wide. Building work started here early in the reign of Darius, probably around 518 BC, soon after or possibly even at the same time as that at Susa, and after Darius' reign probably continued for much of the Achaemenid period. The most active later builders, however, were Xerxes, Artaxerxes I and Artaxerxes III.

Access to the Persepolis terrace was by a double staircase, after which the visitor would have passed through the Gate of All Nations (fig. 35), consisting of two pairs of colossal human-headed winged bulls facing in opposite directions with four columns between them with bull protome capitals. The winged bulls are derived from Assyrian art, but here the bulls have four legs (as opposed to five in Assyria) and the shape of the wings is different. Above the bulls are trilingual inscriptions of Xerxes in Old Persian, Elamite and Babylonian.

Many of the buildings on the Persepolis terrace (fig. 36) have columned halls and columned porticoes (the so-called 'apadana' plan). These include the Hall of 100 Columns, the 'Harem', the Central Building, the Palace of Xerxes, Palace H, the Palace of Darius and the Apadana. The column capitals are of four types (figs 37 and 38), with bulls, lions, griffins and human-headed bulls. Often the door-jambs bear carved decoration, as in the Hall of 100 Columns (figs 39 and 40), the Central Building, the Palaces of Xerxes and Darius (fig. 41) and the 'Harem'. This decoration takes the form of the king or 'Persian hero figure' fighting a bull, a lion, or a griffin; the king with the crown

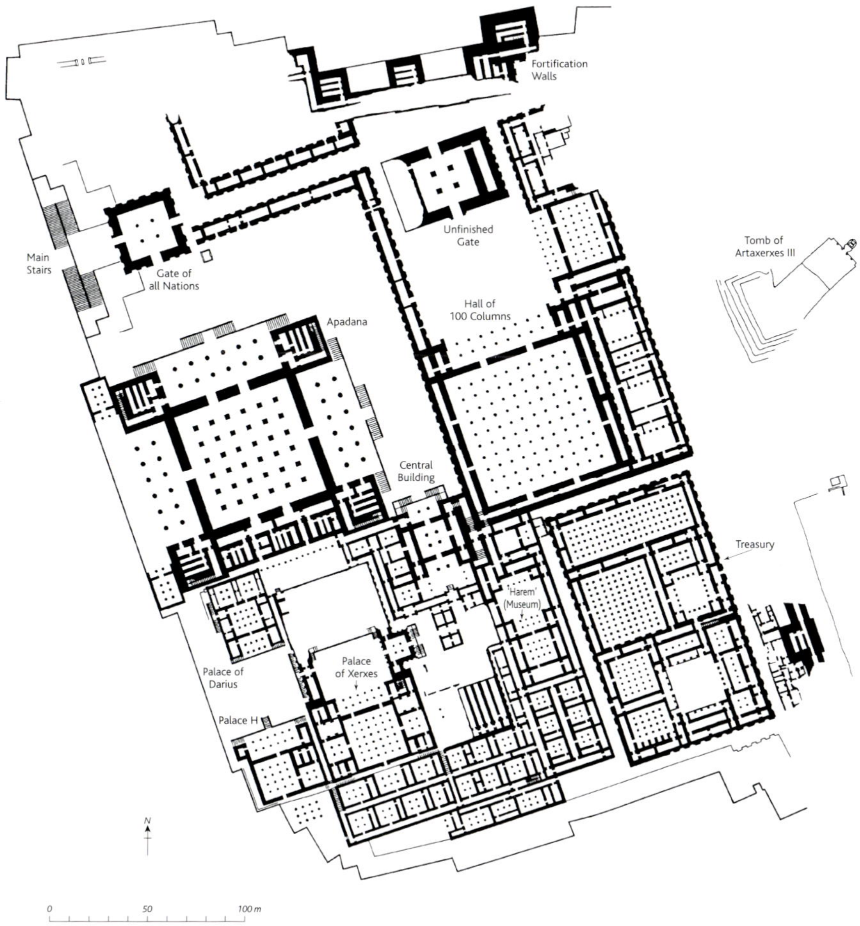

36 (left) Plan of the terrace at Persepolis showing the principal buildings.

37 (below) Double bull column capital, probably from one of the porticoes of the Apadana at Persepolis, 5th century BC.

38 (below) Column capital in the form of back-to-back griffin protomes, probably from the Unfinished Gate at Persepolis, 5th century BC.

prince or attendants; attendants on their own or throne-bearers holding up the enthroned king who sits under a canopy above which hovers the figure in the winged disc (fig. 42). The throne-bearers are either guards in Persian or Median costume or subject peoples from around the empire. There are particularly splendid examples of these decorated door-jambs in the Hall of 100 Columns.

Some of the palaces are raised on platforms and have staircases with carved decoration on the walls and parapets. Such decoration can be found on the Palaces of Darius and Xerxes, the Central Building, Palace H and the Apadana. The motifs include figures climbing staircases and bearing food, drink and live animals; Persian guards; Persian and Median nobles; sphinxes; and

39 Stone relief in a doorway of the Hall of 100 Columns at Persepolis showing an enthroned king, probably Xerxes, mounted on a gigantic platform with lion's paws supported by people from around the empire. 5th century BC.

40 Stone relief in a doorway of the Hall of 100 Columns at Persepolis showing the enthroned king with attendants and below files of guards. 5th century BC.

41 (facing page, bottom) The south side of the Palace of Darius at Persepolis showing files of guards and the lion and bull combat scene.

42 Stone relief in a doorway of the Central Building at Persepolis showing the king with attendants. 5th–4th century BC.

43 Stone relief showing a figure wearing a Median trouser-suit and hood climbing a staircase. He is carrying a covered goblet and may be a priest. This relief comes from the Palace of Darius but dates from the reign of Artaxerxes III (359–338 BC). British Museum (BM 118868, 75 x 40 cm, thickness 13 cm).

lions attacking bulls. There has been discussion about the identity and function of the figures climbing staircases (fig. 43), with opinions ranging from servants carrying provisions for a banquet to priests carrying offerings for a religious ceremony. Recently, Shahrokh Razmjou has argued persuasively in favour of the latter interpretation.

The finest and most spectacular friezes, however, are on the north and east facades of the Apadana. The Apadana, or 'Audience Palace', is the largest columned hall structure known from ancient Iran. It was started by Darius and completed by Xerxes (fig. 44). The columns of the Apadana Palace are 20 m high (fig. 45) and

44 (left) Gold and silver plates from a stone foundation box buried beneath the Apadana at Persepolis. They have trilingual inscriptions of Darius (522–486 BC) in Old Persian, Elamite and Babylonian. Each text begins 'Darius the great king, king of kings, king of countries, son of Hystaspes, an Achaemenian.' National Museum of Iran.

45 (below) Reconstructed drawing of a stone column from Persepolis. The capital is in the form of back-to-back bull protomes, separated from a palm-tree capital by elaborate volutes. The column base is bell-shaped.

46 (below) Stone column from the southern portico of the Apadana at Persepolis. The fluted column shaft between the base and the capital would originally have been much taller. 5th century BC. National Museum of Iran (397, 3.7 m x 1.9 m).

47 (facing page) File of guardsmen armed with spears from the north side of the Apadana at Persepolis. 5th century BC. British Museum (BM 118838, h. 60 cm, l. 107 cm).

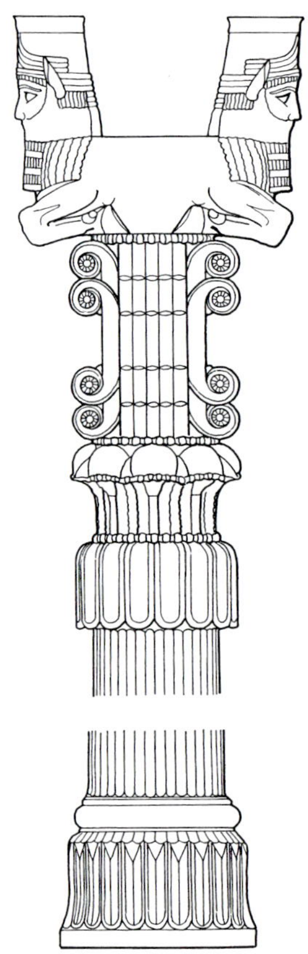

have very elaborate tops (fig. 46) consisting of pendant leaves, palm fronds and double volute decoration, surmounted by bull protome (front part) or lion protome capitals. On the north and east sides of the Apadana are monumental staircases with relief decoration that are mirror images of each other. The two decorative schemes are therefore the same, but in one case reversed.

The reliefs show Iranian nobles, with figures in Persian and Median dress alternating, Persian guardsmen (the Immortals) and the king's chariots with grooms (fig. 47). In the centre originally were panels showing the king seated on a throne, but these were removed at some stage (perhaps in the reign of Artaxerxes II) and replaced by panels with soldiers flanked by panels showing a lion attacking a bull. In addition to the scenes of people at the Persian court, each wing has images of twenty-three delegations of subject peoples bringing presents for the great king. Each group is introduced by an usher in Persian or Median costume and separated by cypress trees (figs 48–50). The members of each delegation are dressed in their national costume, and they bring gifts that are presumably typical of their regions. These representations are therefore of extraordinary interest, and have the potential to tell us a great deal about the different parts of the empire. For example, six of the missions bring horses from what are presumably good horse-breeding areas. It is significant that the members of all six horse-bearing delegations wear trousers, underlining the clear association of the wearing of trousers with the riding of horses.

There has been much discussion about the purpose of Persepolis. Why was this city built? Was it a vanity project conceived by Darius or did it have a real administrative or even religious function? It used to be believed that the city existed just for the celebration of the annual Nowruz (New Year) festival at the time of the spring equinox, but this seems scarcely credible and the large archives of administrative tablets, written in Elamite, found around the Fortification Walls and in the Treasury, show that activity at Persepolis lasted all the year round. It also used to be believed that there was no evidence at Persepolis for residential and

48 (right) Some of the tribute delegations shown on the Apadana reliefs at Persepolis bringing presents for the king. From the top, they are Lydians, Cappadocians, Ionians, Parthians and Indians. Early 5th century BC. Drawing by Ann Searight.

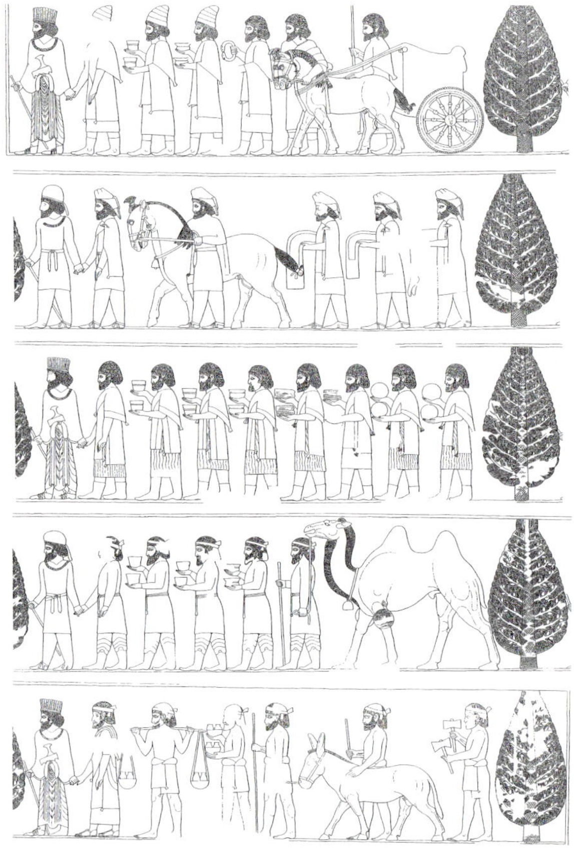

49 (below) Reliefs on the north side of the Apadana at Persepolis showing some of the delegations bringing presents for the king. The delegation at the bottom right is from Lydia.

commercial quarters, but it is now clear that there are extensive and as of yet unexcavated building remains in the plain to the south of the platform. The most likely explanation is that Darius wanted a prestigious new centre on the Iranian plateau to rival or exceed Pasargadae, which had been founded by Cyrus. In this sense, it was a new Persian 'capital' but it is clear that neither Darius nor any other king spent all his time there. In a way, the city probably served multiple functions; it was a capital when the king was in residence, but it also had religious and

50 Reliefs on the north side of the Apadana at Persepolis. These reliefs have been exposed for many centuries and are now in much worse condition than the comparable reliefs on the east side of the Apadana that were exposed in the 1930s.

51 (bottom) Rock-cut tombs of the Persian kings at Naqsh-i Rustam near Persepolis.

administrative functions that lasted all the year round. Nevertheless, it must be admitted that the true picture is still not quite clear, as the tablets seem to belong only to the reigns of Darius, Xerxes and Artaxerxes I. However that may be, Persepolis remained an important centre until the end of the Achaemenid period, when it was captured, looted and destroyed by Alexander. There were probably particularly rich pickings in the Treasury, which must have been a repository of vast wealth, and many important objects remained to be found in the destruction level here by later excavators.

On the slopes of the mountain overlooking Persepolis are rock-cut tombs thought to belong to Artaxerxes II and Artaxerxes III, and there are similar tombs in the cliff at Naqsh-i Rustam (figs 1 and 51) 12 km northwest of Persepolis belonging to Darius the Great, Xerxes, Artaxerxes I and probably Darius II. These tombs have chambers cut into the rock, accessible through a small doorway, and a carved façade which shows the great king in front of a fire altar while the winged disc figure hovers above. The king stands on a gigantic throne that is supported by figures representing subject peoples from around the

52 (facing page) Part of the Ecbatana mound at Hamadan. This is thought to be the site of the ancient Median and Achaemenid city, but no buildings from these periods have yet been discovered.

empire. Facing the royal tombs at Naqsh-i Rustam is a tower-like structure of black and white stone with blind windows (known as the Kabah-i Zardusht or cube of Zoroaster) that probably had a religious function; it is comparable to the Zendan-i Sulaiman at Parargadae).

Hamadan

According to Herodotus (*Histories* 1.98) Hamadan (Ecbatana) was the capital of the Medes at least from the time of a ruler called Deioces onwards, but there is no corroborative evidence for this. It is uncertain whether Hamadan is mentioned in contemporary Assyrian royal inscriptions, but in Babylonian tablets dating from the reigns of Cyrus and Darius there are several references to Hamadan (Agmatanu), one of the texts mentioning that its was visited by a Babylonian businessman during a trip to Iran. By the time of Darius it was undoubtedly an important centre even if it had not been so earlier, as it was here (according to his Bisitun inscription) that Darius executed Phraortes and the Median rebels (see p. 21). In contrast to these few references to Hamadan in Assyrian, Babylonian and Achaemenid sources, there is much about Hamadan in the works of the classical authors. Xenophon and others report that the Achaemenid kings spent the summer months of the year at Ecbatana and the cooler months elsewhere. Herodotus, Diodorus Siculus and Arrian are amongst those who refer to the wealth of Hamadan. It is also mentioned as a mustering place for troops.

From an archaeological perspective, traces of Median and Achaemenid Hamadan remain elusive. Nineteenth-century travellers refer to pieces of column and column bases in different parts of Hamadan, and there are a number of similar pieces on display in the site museum on the Ecbatana mound, but few if any of these seem to have been in their original positions when found.

There are six inscribed column bases or fragments that certainly or probably come from Hamadan (including cat. no. 5), but the exact provenance of only one of them is known. This is a fragment found during Iranian excavations on the Ecbatana mound in a secondary context. The six inscriptions all belong to one or two inscriptions of Artaxerxes II (404–359) which refer to the building of a palace. It seems certain, then, that there was at least a palace (or palaces) of Artaxerxes II at Hamadan; further evidence for the existence of a palace is provided by the discovery during road works at Hamadan of a fragment of a bull capital of typical Achaemenid type. There may also have been a temple dedicated to the goddess Anahita at Hamadan, as alluded to by the classical authors. Thus, Berossus records that Artaxerxes II set up statues

of Anahita in Hamadan and various other places. Frustratingly, however, we do not know the whereabouts of the palace or the putative temple. Iranian excavations on the Ecbatana mound (fig. 52), long supposed to be the site of the ancient city, have uncovered only extensive buildings of the Parthian period, beneath which are some Early Iron Age remains and bedrock. It seems, then that we will have to look elsewhere in Hamadan for the Median and Achaemenid city so graphically described by Polybius in his *Histories*: 'Ecbatana …had always been the royal residence of the Medes and is said to have greatly exceeded all the other cities in wealth and the magnificence of its buildings.'

About 12 km south-west of Hamadan, at a place called Ganj Nameh ('Story of the Treasure') (fig. 53), are two important rock inscriptions of Darius and Xerxes. Each inscription is in a rectangular panel and is arranged in three columns, in Old Persian, Elamite and Babylonian.

Babylon

As we have seen, in 539 BC Cyrus captured Babylon (figs 54 and 55), the ancient city that at least since the time of Hammurabi (1792–1750 BC) had been the foremost political and religious centre in southern Mesopotamia. More recently, it had been the centre of the Neo-Babylonian dynasty and the principal seat of Babylonian kings such as Nebuchadnezzar and Nabonidus. According to classical sources the Persian kings spent several months of the year in Babylon, and we know from archives of cuneiform tablets that Babylon prospered under the Persian kings, even though there were occasional revolts here. It is therefore surprising that there is not more evidence for building activity at Babylon in the Persian period.

There is, however, a small columned hall (fig. 56), no larger than a pavilion, of characteristic Iranian design on the west side of the Southern Palace of Nebuchadnezzar (the so-called Persian

building). There were red concrete-like floors of the type also found at Susa and Persepolis. This building used to be attributed to Darius but is now believed to date from the reign of Artaxerxes II. Glazed bricks and a badly damaged column capital in the form of bull protomes found nearby must have come from this building.

Particularly interesting from our point of view are some fragments of a round-topped stele found at Babylon. It replicates part of the design of the Bisitun relief showing Darius with his foot on a prostrate Gaumata with two rebel kings roped together in front of him, and the text on the reverse apparently reproduces the Babylonian version (or part of it) of the Bisitun inscription, showing that copies were distributed around the empire.

Presumably the Babylonian palaces were lived in by the Persian kings, but the Belgian archaeologist Herrmann Gasche goes further than this and suggests that there was extensive rebuilding of them in the Persian period. He cites as evidence for this architectural features such as the rooms with four pilasters ('salles à quatre saillants'), a device for roofing over a large space, which he believes must have been introduced from

Iran. He concludes that the western part of the Southern Palace was constructed or remodelled in the time of Cyrus and Darius, and that there was also extensive Persian building work in the Northern Palace and the Summer Palace.

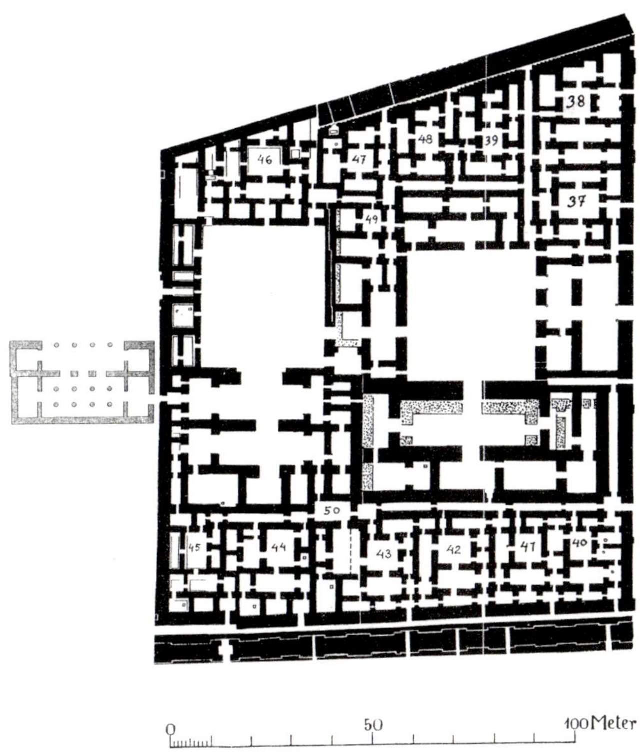

53 (facing page top) Rock-cut panels at Ganj Nameh near Hamadan with trilingual cuneiform inscriptions in Old Persian, Elamite and Babylonian, dating from the reigns of Darius (left) and Xerxes (right). The inscriptions in both panels begin with praises to Ahuramazda.

54 (facing page bottom) View of the site of Babylon showing the restored Southern Palace of Nebuchadnezzar (605–562 BC).

55 (above) View across Babylon with the River Euphrates in the foreground and the Summer Palace mound in the far distance.

56 (right) Plan of the western part of the Southern Palace of Nebuchadnezzar at Babylon and adjoining it on the west side the Persian Building with a columned hall.

Catalogue: Part 2

New Forms of Writing

5 Fragment of column base with Old Persian inscription

404–359 BC, Achaemenid period
Found in Hamadan, Iran before 1885
Dark grey limestone

L. 51.0 cm, H. 10.0 cm, W. 16.5 cm
BM 90855 (1893,1014.54)

This fragment from the *torus* (the bulbous part) of a column base has the left-hand side of a seven-line Old Persian inscription and the right-hand side of a five-line Babylonian inscription of Artaxerxes II (404–359 BC). The column base would originally have been inscribed in three languages (Elamite, Old Persian and Babylonian) and the complete inscription would have read:

> Saith Artaxerxes the great king, king of kings, king of countries, king in this earth, son of Darius the king, of Darius (who was) son of Artaxerxes the king, of Artaxerxes (who was) son of Xerxes the king, of Xerxes (who was) son of Darius the king, of Darius (who was) son of Hystaspes, an Achaemenian. By the favour of Ahuramazda, Anahita and Mithra, this palace (*apadana*) I built. May Ahuramazda, Anahita and Mithra protect me from all evil, and that which I have built may they not shatter or harm.

The Old Persian cuneiform script was devised, apparently in the time of Darius I (522–486 BC), for writing the Old Persian language. The cuneiform (wedge-shaped) script had been used from about 3000 BC onwards to write various languages, principally Sumerian and then Akkadian (Assyrian and Babylonian) in Mesopotamia, but also Hittite (in Turkey), Urartian (in Armenia) and Elamite (in south-west Iran). Now, however, different shaped signs with different values were invented for writing a language that had not previously been written down. Old Persian was an Indo-European language that is an indirect ancestor of modern Persian. It was the language of one branch of the Iranians who settled on the Iranian plateau from about 1500 BC onwards. In the new Old Persian script there are forty-four signs, consisting of a mixture of syllables, vowels and ideograms with a word-divider. Inscriptions survive from the reigns of Darius, Xerxes, Artaxerxes I, Darius II, Artaxerxes II and Artaxerxes III. Inscriptions apparently predating the reign of Darius are probably either the work of later kings or modern forgeries. Inscriptions in Old Persian are mainly monumental, on rock faces (as at Bisitun and Ganj Nameh), on stone reliefs (as at Persepolis) and on column bases, but they also occur on small objects such as cylinder seals (see cat. no. 14), bowls and alabastrons (fig. 33). Generally, Old Persian inscriptions occur alongside Elamite, Babylonian and sometimes hieroglyphic inscriptions all containing the same text. Old Persian inscriptions died out after the collapse of the Achaemenid empire, but Akkadian cuneiform continued in use until the 2nd century AD.

A good start with the decipherment of Old Persian cuneiform was made by the German schoolmaster Georg Friedrich Grotefend (1775–1853) using copies made by early travellers of inscriptions at Persepolis (see fig. 61) and Ganj Nameh near Hamadan (fig. 53), and further progress was made possible when Henry Creswicke Rawlinson (1810–95) copied the great trilingual inscription of Darius at Bisitun between 1835 and (figs 6 and 7). The copying of the Bisitun inscription also made possible the decipherment of Babylonian and Elamite. Apart from Rawlinson, another key figure in the early history of decipherment was the Irish clergyman Edward Hincks (1792–1866).

45035

6

Pottery ostracon with Aramaic inscription

c. 475 BC, Achaemenid period
Probably from Elephantine in Egypt
Pottery

H. 6.7 cm, W. 13.7 cm
BM 45035 (1907,0112.1645)

This potsherd has a painted Aramic inscription in five lines on both sides. On the concave side the inscription reads, 'Greetings to Micaiah from Nathan son of Gemariah. Now, come, enter tomorrow without fail! Lo, it is wages for me/him for tomorrow. Now do not fail to come tomorrow', and on the convex side: 'Greetings [to] Micaiah from Jedaniah. Now, lo, I sent [word] to you yesterday in the name of Hodaviah son of Zechariah, saying, "Come this day", but you did not come. In[to] the hand of [i.e. through] my daughters send [word] to me [or, I sent to you]'.

This ostracon (inscribed potsherd) is similar to about thirty others that were written around 475 BC and apparently deal with movements by boat between Syene and Elephantine in Egypt. Each place was garrisoned by units of Aramaean and Judaean soldiers respectively who served with the Persian army and lived there with their families.

Aramaic is a north-west Semitic language related to Phoenician and Hebrew that was written in an alphabetic script with twenty-two characters. Because Aramaic was so much easier to read and write than the very cumbersome cuneiform writing systems, it began to be used in the Assyrian and Babylonian empires alongside cuneiform for administration and communication. Amongst the early uses of Aramaic in Assyria was as fitters' marks on glazed bricks from Nimrud, discovered in 1989 by a British Museum expedition to Nimrud. The bricks are dated to the reign of Shalmaneser III (858–824 BC) through cuneiform inscriptions of that king. Aramaic was therefore in use before the Achaemenid period, even in Iran, but it became more widespread in the time of the Persian kings. It was often written on perishable materials such as parchment and leather, but also on potsherds (as the present example), stone vessels and utensils, and Aramaic letters were sometimes incised on metal objects and stone seals. In many respects Aramaic became the *lingua franca* of the Persian empire, and seems to have been in widespread use. We even find an echo of this in the Bible, where it is recorded that 'in the days of Artaxerxes king of Persia, Bishlam, Mithredath, Tabeel and the rest of his associates wrote a letter to Artaxerxes [about the rebuilding of the temple in Jerusalem]. The letter was written in Aramaic script and in the Aramiac language' (Ezra 4, v. 7).

Catalogue: Part 3

A New Religion

7

Oxus Treasure plaque with embossed and chased decoration showing a priest

5th–4th century BC, Achaemenid
Oxus Treasure; A.W. Franks bequest 1897
Gold

H. 15.1 cm, W. 7.5 cm, Wt 82.73 g
BM 123949 (1897,1231.48)

This plaque shows a male figure facing right, wearing a belted knee-length tunic over trousers. On his head he has a hood, evidently of some soft material, with a neck-guard at the back. This is the so-called 'Median costume'. His chin and perhaps also his mouth are covered apparently by a separate piece of material. Above this, a moustache is clearly visible. On his thigh he wears a Persian short sword (*akinakes*) in a scabbard, and in his right hand he carries a bundle of sticks or a *barsom*. The two ends of the belt hang down at the front, showing it is made of rope or cloth. His tunic is decorated with bands of embroidery or applied material. Two such bands run vertically down the length of the tunic, and there are further bands on the bottom hem of the tunic, at the wrists and forming an inverted T-shape on the upper arm. Similarly decorated costumes can be seen worn by tribute peoples shown on the relief decoration of the Palace of Darius (*tachara*) at Persepolis, both on the central panel of the western stairway and on the southern flight of the western stairway (fig. 61). In both cases the inverted T-shape on the upper arm is clearly visible. The inscription in Old Persian in the middle of the central panel dates from the time of Artaxerxes III (359–338 BC), so it is presumed that the surrounding reliefs also date from his reign. The figures wearing similar costumes to the gold plaque bring bracelets, a folded costume and bowls. They cannot be paralleled exactly on the Apadana reliefs or on the tomb reliefs at Naqsh-i Rustam, but they closely resemble the various groups of Scythians, some of whom may have lived in the area where the Oxus Treasure is believed to have been found. There is also an ivory plaque from Susa that shows a figure wearing a belted tunic of Median type with vertical decorative bands at the sides, and an actual example of such a costume was found in the burial of a warrior in the Issyk kurgan (burial mound) in Kazakhstan.

The first question is what does this figure represent? Amongst the 180 gold and silver objects that make up the Oxus Treasure there are about fifty gold plaques (fig. 57) with figural representations, of which this is one, all except three showing human figures. Of these, twenty-five of the plaques show male figures wearing trouser suits and hoods, occasionally with the addition of an overcoat (*kandys*), and holding a *barsom*. The present example has probably the best-executed design, with some of the representations being extremely crude and sometimes very lightly incised. The presence of all these gold plaques in the Treasure has often led to assumptions that the Treasure must have been votive, in other words the objects were presented to a temple. If this is so, the temple was presumably in the vicinity of Takht-i

57 Selection of gold votive plaques from the Oxus Treasure showing male figures wearing Median trouser-suits and hoods and carrying *barsoms* (bundles of sticks). They are probably priests. 5th–4th century BC. British Museum. Drawings by Ann Searight.

58 (left) Two gold figurines from the Oxus Treasure showing men wearing Median trouser-suits, hoods and overcoats and carrying bundles of sticks (*barsoms*). 5th–4th century BC. British Museum (BM 123903 and 123902, h. 5.3 cm and 5.6 cm).

59 (below) Gilded silver figure from the Oxus Treasure of a bearded man wearing a Persian style dress. He is holding in his left hand either a bundle of sticks (*barsom*) or a flower. 5th–4th century BC. British Museum (BM 123901, h. 14.8 cm).

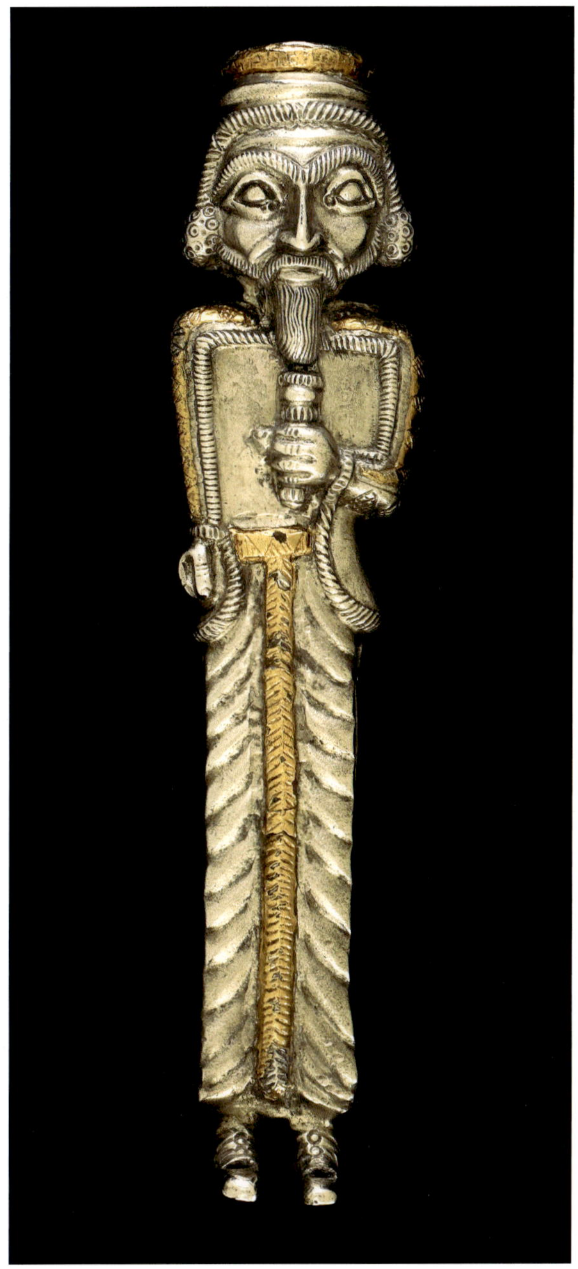

Kuwad, on the north bank of the River Oxus in modern Tajikistan, but as the Treasure was retrieved by villagers and not recovered in a proper archaeological excavation, we have no information on this point.

About twenty-five of the figures in Median dress are carrying the bundles of sticks or twigs that are known as *barsoms*. There are also in the Treasure two small solid gold statuettes (fig. 58) showing figures dressed in Median trouser suits with overcoats and holding *barsoms*. Another larger figure in silver (fig. 59) wearing the Persian costume of long dress with pleated folds also shows a man holding what appears to be a *barsom*, but it has been convincingly suggested that this is more likely to be a stylized lotus flower (Moorey 1988, no. 54). *Barsoms* made up of bundles of sticks are associated with ancient Iranian religious ceremonies. The origins of the practice are not clear, but one suggestion is that the twigs represent grasses that were spread around a sacred precinct prior to an animal sacrifice, and after the ceremony a bundle of them was gathered up by the priest. However that may be, the *barsom* came in due course to be associated with the Zoroastrian religion, and was held by officiating priests as well as by individuals making sacrifices. It may also be that the *barsom* was sometimes a mark of piety. It is significant that in the case of the Oxus Treasure *barsoms* are only certainly being held by figures wearing Median dress, as we know that the *magi* (priests) during the Achaemenid period were Median. The combined attributes of Median dress and *barsom* have inevitably led to suggestions that the figures in the Oxus Treasure are priests, and possibly even Zoroastrian priests. It may going too far to suggest that they are all priests, and perhaps it is rather unlikely, but is certainly possible that they could all be members of a priestly caste. We are perhaps on firmer ground with the associations of the *barsom*, which seem to point to the Zoroastrian religion or an early version of it. What significance this may have for the postulated temple to which the Oxus Treasure objects are thought to have been presented is unclear; evidently it could have had Zoroastrian or pre-Zoroastrian associations.

We now turn to the vexed question of whether the Achaemenid kings were followers of Zoroastrianism. This is the religion of ancient Iranian origin that takes its name from the prophet Zarathushtra (Greek Zoroaster) who reformed it. Traditionally, the lifetime of Zoroaster is dated to the period 628–551 BC, but many scholars now believe he flourished much earlier than this, perhaps in the period 1400–1200 BC. In either case, he is closely associated with eastern Iran and Central Asia.

In the Zoroastrian religion, Ahuramazda is the creator of everything that is good, but he is opposed by an evil sprit who represents everything that is bad, named Angra Mainyu, or Ahriman. These two opposed forces are represented by truth or order (*asha*) and the lie (*diruj*), or disorder. For Zoroastrians, good thoughts, good words and good deeds are the guiding principles of their religion. Ahuramazda himself is the creator of everything, but he is assisted by six radiant beings that together with Ahuramazda himself make up the Amesha Spentas, the Bounteous Immortals. The radiant beings are good thought, righteousness, devotion, dominion, wholeness and immortality. Each together with Ahuramazda is responsible for protecting one of the seven holy creations that include fire and water. For this reason both fire and water have a special place in the religion,

7 Plaque with embossed and chased decoration showing a priest

and fires are kept constantly alight in the main Zoroastrian temples. The Amesha Spentas in turn evoked other beneficent divinities that are referred to as the Yazatas, or Worshipful Ones. The Yazatas rank third in the heavenly council after Ahuramazda and the Bounteous Immortals. Amongst them are well-known figures such as Mithra, whose cult later spread across the Roman empire, and Anahita, who was assimilated by the classical authors with Aphrodite.

One of the characteristic features of Zoroastrianism is the method of burial, which prevents dead bodies from coming into contact with the earth, which is a sacred element. This is achieved by exposing bodies to be excarnated by wild beasts and birds of prey. The bones are then collected and then placed in an ossuary. In modern times, excarnation takes place on so-called Towers of Silence in India.

So, what of the Achaemenid kings? They did not themselves leave any descriptions of their own religious practices, so let us look first at the description by the Greek historian Herodotus who lived in the 5th century BC (*c*. 484–425 BC):

> As to the usages of the Persians, I know them to be these. It is not their custom to make and set up statues and temples and altars, but those who make such they deem foolish, as I suppose, because they never believed the gods, as do the Greeks, to be in the likeness of men; but they call the whole circle of heaven Zeus [presumably Ahuramazda], and to him they offer sacrifice on the highest peaks of the mountains; they sacrifice also to the sun and moon and earth and fire and water and winds. These are the only gods to whom they have ever sacrificed from the beginning; they have learnt later, to sacrifice to the "heavenly" Aphrodite, from the Assyrians and Arabians… And this is their fashion of sacrifice to the aforesaid gods: when about to sacrifice they neither build altars nor kindle fire, they use no libations, nor music, nor fillets, nor barley meal; but to whomsoever of the gods a man will sacrifice, he leads the beast to an open space and then calls on the god… He then cuts the victim limb from limb into portions, and having boiled the flesh spreads the softest grass [presumably those that were collected for *barsom* bundles], trefoil by choice, and places all of it on this. When he has so disposed it a Magian comes near and chants over it the song of the birth of the gods, as the Persian tradition relates it; for no sacrifice can be offered without a Magian. Then after a little while the sacrificer carries away the flesh and uses it as he pleases (*Histories*, Book I, 131–2).

60 Large stone slab from Persepolis with the so-called 'Daiva' inscription of Xerxes (486-465 BC) in Old Persian cuneiform. Here, Xerxes lists the countries of which he was king, and says that in one of them false gods (*daivas*) were worshipped. He replaced them with the worship of Ahuramazda and Arta (order or truth). National Museum of Iran (16, 53 x 52 cm, thickness 10 cm).

Herodotus also makes reference (Book I, 140) to burial customs:

> The dead bodies of Persians are not buried before they have been mangled by bird or dog. That this is the way of the Magians I know for a certainty; for they do not conceal the practice. But this is certain, that before the Persians bury the body in earth they embalm it in wax.

Berossus, a Babylonian priest writing in Greek at the beginning of the 3rd century BC, whose history is only partly preserved in the works of other writers, also wrote that originally the Persians had no images, but claims that Artaxerxes II introduced the practice by setting up statues of Aphrodite (Anahita) in various cities including Persepolis, Susa, Babylon and Ecbatana.

There is much here that can be equated with Zoroastrianism, or an early form of the religion, although modern Zoroastrians insist that animal sacrifice was never a part of the religion. However that may be, the reverence for the elements, the idea of outdoor worship and the exposure of dead bodies, all find reflections in Zoroastrianism.

Foremost amongst the Persian sources are of course the inscriptions of the kings themselves, so let us consider these next. All the Achaemenid kings who have left us inscriptions pay homage to Ahuramazda. Thus Darius, in his great Bisitun inscription (figs 6 and 7), says, 'By the favour of Ahuramazda I am king; Ahuramazda bestowed the kingdom upon me' or 'Whoso shall worship Ahuramazda, divine blessing will be upon him, both (while) living and (when) dead'. He was also at pains to stress that he 'was not a lie-follower' as opposed to the false Gaumata who 'lied to the people'. On the gold and silver plates (fig. 44) that were buried in foundation boxes under the corners of the main hall of the Apadana palace at Persepolis, Darius wrote, 'May Ahuramazda protect me, and my royal house.' At Susa, he recorded, 'A great god is Ahuramazda, who makes excellence in this earth, who makes happiness for man, who makes good horses and good chariots. On me he bestowed them. Me may Ahuramazda protect and what has been built by me [i.e his palace at Susa (fig. 31)].' His son Xerxes continued in the same vein, proclaiming at Persepolis, 'What has been built by me here, and what has been built by me at a distance (from here), all that by

61 (top and bottom) Stone reliefs and an inscription of Artaxerxes III (359–338 BC) on the west side of the Palace of Darius at Persepolis. The reliefs show lion and bull combat scenes and tributaries bringing presents. Drawing by Ann Searight.

7 Plaque with embossed and chased decoration showing a priest

the favour of Ahuramazda I built'. In his so-called Daiva inscription (fig. 60), Xerxes lists the countries of which he was king and says that in one of them false gods (*daivas*) were worshipped. He replaced them with the worship of Ahuramazda and Arta ('order', 'truth'). Following Xerxes, Artaxerxes I, Darius II, Artaxerxes II and Artaxerxes III all talk about accomplishing things with the favour of Ahuramazda and seeking his protection. In his inscriptions at Susa and Hamadan, Artaxerxes II introduces Mithra and Anahita, and Artaxerxes III again refers to Mithra in an inscription added to the Palace of Darius at Persepolis (fig. 61). As we have already seen, following Ahuramazda, Mithra and Anahita were important figures in Zoroastrianism. It is indisputable, then, that at least from the time of Darius onwards Achaemenid kings worshipped

62 (facing page) The Kabah-i Zardusht (the Cube of Zoroaster) at Naqsh-i Rustam. Like the Zendan-i Suleiman at Pasargadae (fig. 20) the purpose of this building is unknown but it probably had a religious function.

Ahuramazda, and that from the time of Artaxerxes II they also recognized Mithra and Anahita. However, whether they can actually be called Zoroastrians is another matter.

To start with, the situation is complicated by references in the royal inscriptions to 'other gods'. Thus at Bisitun, Darius makes reference several times to Ahuramazda and 'the other gods who are'. At Persepolis, he refers to Ahuramazda as 'the greatest of the gods'; we also have references to 'Ahuramazda together with the gods of the royal house'. At Persepolis Xerxes proclaims, 'May Ahuramazda protect me together with the gods.' Of course, it is possible that they are simply referring to other Zoroastrian divine beings such as Mithra and Anahita, but it is also possible that they are alluding to the local or Elamite deities mentioned in cuneiform tablets from Persepolis. Among the Persepolis Fortification Tablets, written between the 13th and 28th year of Darius, are texts dealing with the provision of rations, such as cereals, wine or animals, for religious ceremonies, mostly in the province of Fars. The most frequent of these is the Lan ceremony that had a pre-Achaemenid origin in the Elamite period, and there are also a number or others. Various gods are mentioned in the texts, notably the Elamite god Humban, and other Elamite and even Babylonian deities. However, Iranian gods are also mentioned, including Ahuramazda and Mithra, together with Elamite gods, and it seems that both Iranian and Elamite priests could conduct ceremonies involving gods that were not native to them. Sometimes, both Elamite and Iranian gods are worshipped in the same ceremony. All this implies a good deal of integration, which has led some scholars to see the tablets providing further evidence for the process of Elamite–Persian acculturation, during which the Achaemenids absorbed and took over many elements of Elamite civilization and culture including religious practices and beliefs. The result was that the pantheon of Fars took on a 'Persian' aspect that included both Elamite and Iranian elements. Others would argue that the funding of ceremonies involving Elamite gods, even when they appear alongside Iranian deities, does not necessarily mean that the Achaemenid kings themselves believed in them or viewed them as being on a par with their own Iranian deities. The matter remains unresolved and it may be inappropriate to try to enumerate a 'pantheon' in an environment where religious regulation was probably alien.

We should also remember that the Achaemenid kings were happy to acknowledge other gods when convenient or appropriate. For example, on the statue of Darius, made in Egypt and brought to Susa in antiquity, the trilingual

7 Plaque with embossed and chased decoration showing a priest

cuneiform inscriptions (in Old Persian, Elamite and Babylonian) pay homage to Ahuramazda and ask for his protection. The hieroglyphic text, on the other hand, pays homage to the Egyptian gods Re, the sun-god, and Atum, the creator god, and makes no mention of Ahuramazda. Similarly, although we have no direct evidence for Cyrus' support of Ahuramazda, it is worth remembering that when he captured Babylon, it was the Babylonian god Marduk who 'took the hand of Cyrus, king of the city of Anshan, and called him by his name, proclaiming him aloud for the kingship over all of everything'. There is no mention here of Ahuramazda.

What can be concluded from all this? It has to be admitted that the evidence is contradictory. There is no doubt that the Achaemenid kings worshipped Ahuramazda, and in his Bisitun inscription Darius makes a point of saying that the Elamites and (more surprisingly) the Scythians did *not* respect Ahuramazda (sections 72, 75). However, the Achaemenid kings may also have been ready to pay homage to certain non-Iranian gods. They certainly did as a matter of exigency, particularly when travelling abroad. Also, although the royal tomb facades at Naqsh-i Rustam (fig. 62) and Persepolis show the king involved in a ritual that may be Zoroastrian

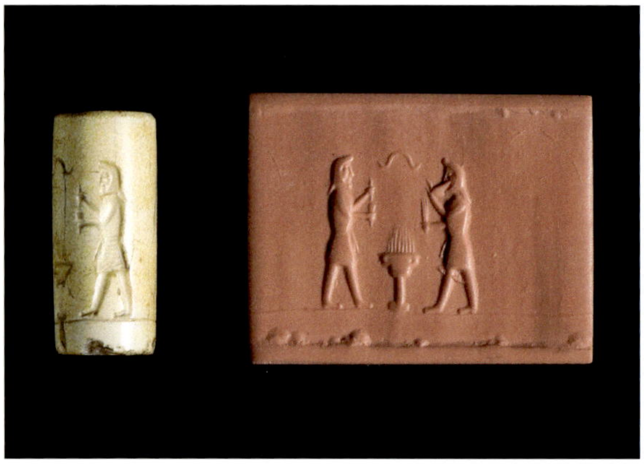

63 Cylinder seal showing figures in Median dress on either side of a flaming altar. The figure on the left holds a pestle and mortar, and that on the right holds a *barsom*. 5th–4th century BC. British Museum (BM 89528, 2.65 x 1.1 cm).

(paying homage to the sacred fire beneath the winged disc, probably a symbol of the god-given glory or *khvarnah*), the method of burial, placing the body in a rock-cut tomb, is not Zoroastrian. Even here, though, some authorities have argued that placing bodies in rock-cut tombs (or a freestanding tomb in the case of Cyrus) is a way of preventing the body coming into contact with the earth. Lastly, we have no evidence that the Achaemenid kings were aware of the teachings of Zoroaster. They certainly do not mention him, although in itself this may not be significant as he is not mentioned either in later Sasanian period official inscriptions (see p. 93). On the whole, the balance of evidence seems to point to the Achaemenid kings being followers of Ahuramazda and the unreformed ancient Iranian religion, that is before it had been restructured and codified by Zoroaster. For this reason they are often called Mazda worshippers, a term used to indicate people who worshipped Ahuramazda without being Zoroastrian in the proper sense of the word.

Whether or not the Achaemenid kings themselves were Zoroastrian there seems little doubt that the Zoroastrian religion took root in Iran during the Achaemenid period. Apart from the representations on the royal tombs at Naqsh-i Rustam and Persepolis, there are sundry indications from around the empire. For example, there is a limestone altar from Bünyän near Kayseri in Turkey, now in the Ankara Museum, which has on the sides a representation of a priest in Median trouser suit with overcoat and holding a *barsom*. A fragmentary stone relief from Daskyleion, also in Turkey, shows two priests (*magi*) with covered mouths dressed in trouser suits and hoods and holding *barsoms*, standing in front of an altar on which are the heads of sacrificed animals. There are also a number of seals featuring fire altars, including one in the British Museum (fig. 63) that shows two figures wearing Median trouser suits on either side of a flaming altar. The figure on the left holds a pestle and mortar and the figure on the right a *barsom*. Pestles and mortars have been found at Persepolis, sometimes with Aramaic inscriptions, showing they were probably used in religious ceremonies.

We are thus entitled to talk about the introduction of a new religion at this time. The Zoroastrian tradition was kept alive during the ensuing Hellenistic period, and in Parthian times it seems to have flourished. From this period, we have the testimony of the Greek author Strabo:

> They also have *pyraetheia* [fire temples], noteworthy enclosures; and in the midst of these there is an altar, on which there i… large quantity of ashes and where the … keep the fire ever burning. And there, en… daily, they make incantations for about an hour, holding before the fire a bundle of rods and wearing round their heads high turbans of felt, which reach down over their cheeks far enough to cover their lips.

According to legend, it was also during the Parthian period, in the reign of Vologases I (*c.* 51–78 AD), that the different parts of the Avesta, the Zoroastrian holy books containing the teachings of Zoroaster, were gathered together. According to Zoroastrian tradition, the original manuscript of the Avesta was burnt by Alexander, for which sacrilegious act he is known as the accursed (*gojastak*). In the Sasanian period (3rd–7th century AD), Zoaroastrianism effectively became the state religion, but although there was much forcible conversion, particularly in the time of the high priest Kartir in the 3rd century AD, for

…of the time Jews, Christians, Manichaeans,
…ans and Buddhists were able, in some
…other, to practise their religions. At this
…sta was written down in its present
…-eastern Iranian language known
…ing Pahlavi (Middle Persian)

…uest of the 7th century AD,
…ad of Islam, there was
…ber of Zoroastrians,
…onvert to the new
re… …ian community
cont… …n around Yazd
in cent… …ans left Iran,
tradition… …d settled
in and arou… … . The
descendants … …as Parsees
or Parsis. The … …s now
in India is in Mu… …ndia,
countries with smal…
include Pakistan, Taji…
Australia, the UK and t…
that the total number of Z…
now fewer than one-quarter…

7 Plaque with embossed and chased decoration showing a priest

Errata

The Cyrus Cylinder and Ancient Persia

The image on page 12 is the title page of Xenophon's *Anabasis*, not the *Cyropaedia*, from the collection of Thomas Jefferson's personal books in the Library of Congress

The first sentence on page 31 should read 'The Cyrus Cylinder is a barrel-shaped clay cylinder that is inscribed in the Babylonian language in Babylonian cuneiform (wedge-shaped script).'

Catalogue: Part 4

A New Form of Currency

8 Gold coin in form of a daric

500–480 BC, Achaemenid
Find-spot unknown, acquired 1919
Gold

Diam. 1.4 cm, Wt 8.37 g
BM 1919,0516.15

Gold coin, showing on the obverse the 'royal archer' (see Commentary below) kneeling with a bow in one hand and a spear in the other.

9 Silver coin in form of a siglos

520–500 BC, Achaemenid
Find-spot unknown, acquired 1852
Silver

Diam. 1.4 cm, Wt 5.4 g
BM 1852,1027.2

Silver coin, showing on the obverse the royal archer (see Commentary below) kneeling and drawing a bow.

10 Silver coin in form of a stater

410–370 BC, Achaemenid
Find-spot unknown, acquired before 1892
Silver

Diam. 2.4 cm, Wt 14.78 g
BM BMC Ionia 323,1

Silver coin, showing on the obverse the royal archer (see Commentary below) kneeling with a bow in one hand and a spear in the other, with Greek letters on either side.

Commentary on cat. nos 8–10

Traditionally in the Ancient Near East gold, silver and even copper were used for purposes of exchange, sometimes in the form of ingots but more often cut into small pieces. This practice continued right down to the beginning of the Achaemenid period (as attested for example at Tepe Nush-i Jan where a hoard of silver currency was found in one of the Median period buildings) and precious metal continued to be used for currency even after the introduction of coins, as can be seen from a hoard found at Babylon where silver bullion is mixed with coins.

The Achaemenid kings were introduced to coinage after Cyrus captured Sardis in 547 or 546 BC. By that time the Lydians had already been using coins for about a century, but their distribution was restricted to western Turkey. The latest Lydian coins are known as croeseids (fig. 64), after Croesus, the last king of Lydia, and they show the foreparts of a lion and a bull confronting each other. This motif of a lion attacking a bull, but showing the complete animals, later became popular at Persepolis. Although the capture of Sardis gave Cyrus control of the Lydian royal mint, croeseids continued to be minted and circulated until the time of Darius. New designs and weight standards were then introduced, and continued in use under Darius' successors. The new coins

had an image of an archer on the obverse and a rectangular depression, or 'incuse', on the back, as the croeseids had done. Over time the image of the archer changed, so that four main types can be recognized, but essentially they all show a figure wearing a crown and holding a bow. This figure is often referred to as 'the royal archer', but whether it is actually the king who is being depicted is hotly disputed by scholars. In Darius' reform of the coinage, two denominations were introduced: the gold daric with a weight of about 8.4 g, which was equivalent to the Mesopotamian shekel, and a silver siglos with a weight of about 5.5 g, which was apparently half the weight of the old silver Croesus stater. There were thus different weight standards for gold and silver, but the exchange rate between the two was fixed. In the 4th century BC the royal mint, perhaps under Greek influence, adopted a heavier weight standard for silver coinage (see cat. no. 10).

Apart from the royal coinage, which was produced in the royal mint at Sardis and perhaps another centre in western Asia Minor, local satraps (provincial governors) in different parts of the empire, but principally Asia Minor, Phoenicia, Samaria and Egypt, minted their own coins, often showing strong Iranian influence but sometimes incorporating Greek features. The result was that during the Achaemenid period coins were widely used in the western part of the Achaemenid empire, but apparently less frequently in the eastern part of the empire, where traditional types of currency may have continued to prevail. However that may be, we can conclude that before the Achaemenid period the use of coins was restricted to part of western Turkey, but under the Persian kings from Darius onwards coins were widely circulated at least in the western part of the Achaemenid empire.

64 (facing page) Gold croeseid stater, minted at Sardis, showing a lion attacking a bull, *c.* 560–540 BC. British Museum (1841,0726.522, diam. 1.6 cm, weight 8.035 g).

Chapter IV

The Art and Architecture of the Persian Empire

Achaemenid Persian art was eclectic, that is to say that it drew on a number of different sources for ideas and inspiration. This seems to be because the Achaemenid Persians rose to power very rapidly, finding themselves in control of what was then a world empire, and were faced with the need to create an official style of art that would be in keeping with the grandeur of the empire. The eclecticism of their art was therefore partly driven by pragmatism, but there must have been another underlying motive, namely to make the subject peoples feel that they were part of the empire, belonged to it and had contributed to it. For the same reasons, the choice of four languages for official inscriptions – Old Persian, Elamite, Babylonian (effectively including Assyrian) and Egyptian – was quite deliberate, and it is no coincidence that these were the traditions – Iranian, Elamite, Mesopotamian and Egyptian – that figure most largely in Achaemenid art and architecture.

The best-known type of Achaemenid building, however, is Iranian in inspiration. This is the columned hall. Such buildings are known at all the major sites in Iran (Persepolis, Pasargadae and Susa), as well as at a number of smaller sites, and there are examples further afield at Babylon and, according to literary evidence, at places like Sidon in the Lebanon. These structures consist of a central columned hall surrounded by columned porticoes usually on three sides, with corner towers. The columns, generally of stone, sit on massive stone bases and support exotic capitals in the form of bulls and other animals. Whether the columned hall was an Iranian invention is not entirely clear, but certainly there are examples in north-west Iran in the late second or early first millennium BC, notably at sites such as Hasanlu (fig. 65), and it seems certain that the Achaemenid columned halls are descended from that tradition. Columned halls are also found in the Arabian Peninsula, and some scholars have suggested that the Achaemenid halls are derived from there, across the Persian Gulf, but it seems unnecessary to look outside Iran for inspiration when such good models are close at hand. The introduction of the columned hall into the architectural repertoire of the Ancient Near East is all the more remarkable when we remember that this was an area previously dominated by buildings that were made exclusively of mud brick, with flat roofs supported by wooden beams.

In the Achaemenid period, the earliest examples of columned halls are at Cyrus' new foundation at Pasargadae. The two palaces, the garden pavilions and the gatehouse are all built with columns. These buildings also made extensive use of stone. As there was no local tradition of constructing large stone buildings, Cyrus turned to foreign workmen for specialist

65 The site of Hasanlu in north-west Iran where early examples of columned halls have been found.

assistance. It is thought that craftsmen, principally stonemasons, were brought in from the newly conquered kingdom of Lydia and from nearby Ionia. Their presence at Pasargadae is attested by a number of technical features in the stonework, for example by the use of claw-toothed picks and chisels, by a particular way of creating tight joints between stone blocks and column drums (*anathyrosis*), by the use of metal dovetail clamps to hold the stone blocks together, by the smooth edges ('drafted margins') on the stone blocks of the Tall-i Takht, and by the column bases with horizontally fluted tori in Palace P. It is also suggested that the Tomb of Cyrus was inspired by Lydian prototypes, but this is less certain. It is true that there was no previous tradition in Iran for this type of tomb, but although such tombs are certainly known in Asia Minor they do not actually predate the Tomb of Cyrus. Another possibility is that the design of the tomb was dictated by a wish to isolate the body from the earth, in partial recognition of Zoroastrian practice. However, foreign influence (from Asia Minor) can again be detected in the construction of the tomb, in the form of the double moulding that is convex above and concave below (*cyma reversa*) and the denticulation (imitation beam ends) under the cornice.

Just as Cyrus enlisted foreign stonemasons for his construction work at Pasargadae, so Darius called on foreign workmen to help with the building of his vast new palace at Susa. In his so-called Foundation Inscription from Susa (fig. 31), he lists the craftsmen who took part, including stonemasons from Ionia and Sardis, goldsmiths from Media and Egypt, carpenters

from Sardis and Egypt and bricklayers from Babylon. Similarly, the materials were brought from around the empire, including cedar from the Lebanon and gold from Turkey and Central Asia. The resulting palace at Susa is a curious bend of Iranian-style columned hall (fig. 66) and Babylonian-style mud brick building. Even in the Babylonian-style part of the building, though, there are Iranian-style touches. Thus the glazed brick friezes, echoing those of the Ishtar Gate at Babylon, are mostly made not of simple mud bricks, as in Babylon and earlier in Assyria, but of a type of sintered quartz. Also, although the decorative schemes on these glazed brick panels were partly derived from Mesopotamia, namely the mythological monsters, the files of Persian archers (fig. 30) are purely Iranian in inspiration.

We find the full flowering of Achaemenid art and architecture at Persepolis. The bulk of the building work here was in the reigns of Darius and Xerxes, but continued for much of the Achaemenid period. The first point to note is that the idea of using stone gateway figures and decorating palaces with stone friezes on a monumental scale clearly comes from Assyria, and indeed Assyrian influence can be first detected at Pasargadae. There, for example, in one of the two palaces we have the bottom parts of doorway reliefs showing Assyrian-style figures such as the lion-demon, the bull-man and the figure wearing a fish-cloak. At Persepolis, Assyrian influence is particularly clear in the colossal human-headed winged bulls in the Gate of All Nations, but there are obvious differences between the

66 (facing page) Stone column drums on the site of Darius' Palace at Susa.

Persepolis bulls and their Assyrian counterparts. For example, the Persepolis bulls have four legs rather than five and wings that are curled at the ends. With regard to the decorative stone friezes, there is a significant difference between Achaemenid Iran and Assyria, in that in Assyria the friezes line the inside walls of rooms of state, while at Persepolis the friezes are on the facades of external staircases (as in the Apadana) or they line gateways (as in the Hall of 100 Columns). Also, the subject matter is generally different. While Assyrian friezes mostly show military campaigns and scenes of hunting, the Persepolis friezes show courtly processions, the bringing of gifts and preparations for ceremonies. There are, however, some points of contact, such as scenes of the king sitting in state, a hero figure in single combat with a monster, and various kinds of hybrid creature. Another similarity between Assyrian and Persian palaces is the use of paint. In both cases the stone reliefs were painted, as were the bare plaster walls in the palaces. The evidence for painted plaster decoration is more extensive in Assyria than in Persia, but although limited there is evidence from Iran at Susa and Pasargadae. Egyptian influence can also be seen at Persepolis, for example in the Egyptian-style feather decoration above the windows and doorways and in the floral ornamentation at the tops of the columns. In spite of the various foreign influences that can be identified, however, the end product is distinctively Persian. Persepolis is an expression of Persian art and architecture that, although undoubtedly eclectic, is in the end distinctive, characteristic and unmistakably Persian. In spite of this, claims still persist that Persepolis is strongly influenced by Greek art. It has even been suggested that Telephanes, a Greek sculptor said by the elder Pliny to have worked for Darius and Xerxes, was the grand master of the Persepolis friezes. In fact, there is possibly more Persian influence in the Parthenon at Athens, rebuilt from 447 BC onwards after an earlier building had been destroyed during the invasion of Xerxes in 480 BC, than there is Greek influence at Persepolis.

With regard to minor arts, the Achaemenid contribution to glyptic art (seals and sealings), jewellery and metal working is discussed in the relevant sections of this catalogue.

Catalogue: Part 5

New Types of Seal

11 Stamp seal with hunting scene

5th–4th century BC, Achaemenid
Find-spot unknown, acquired before 1930
Greyish-blue chalcedony

H. 1.3 cm, (base) 2.0 x 2.8 cm
BM 120326

This seal is engraved with a scene showing a horse and rider wearing a Median-style trouser suit with hood. The rider draws a composite bow and aims an arrow at a leaping goat, which he is pursuing. The rider sits on a saddle-cloth and the horse has a knotted tail.

12 Stamp seal with hero fighting a winged bull

5th–4th century BC, Achaemenid
Find-spot unknown, acquired before 1900
Grey chalcedony

H. 2.5 cm, Diam. 2.0 cm (base)
BM 89893

This seal is engraved with a scene showing a figure wearing a pleated dress and crown (sometimes called the 'Persian royal hero', see Commentary below) holding a sword in one hand and grasping by the throat with the other hand a winged bull standing on its hind legs.

13

Cylinder seal with figures fighting a lion and a bull

6th–5th century BC, Neo-Elamite or Achaemenid
Find-spot unknown, Claudius James Rich collection, acquired 1825
Grey-brown chalcedony

H. 4.9 cm, Diam. 2.25 cm
BM 89337 (1825,0503.136)

This seal is engraved with a scene showing two figures battling with animals. The first figure wears a pleated dress and a crown (the 'Persian royal hero', see Commentary below) and holds a sword in one hand and a lion by its rear leg with the other. The second figure wears a long dress with fringed edges and holds a whip in one hand and a bull by its horn in the other.

14 The Darius cylinder seal

6th–5th century BC, Achaemenid
Obtained in Egypt, acquired 1835
Green and grey-brown clouded chalcedony

H. 3.7 cm, Diam. 1.7 cm
BM 89132 (1835,0630.1)

This famous seal is engraved with a scene showing Darius I (522–486 BC) in his chariot hunting lions, with a winged figure (Ahuramazda or the kingly glory) above. The king is aiming an arrow at a lion which rears up in front of his chariot while another lion is being trampled by the horses. The chariot is similar to the model gold chariot in the Oxus Treasure and to royal chariots shown on the Apadana reliefs at Persepolis, and is pulled by two small horses. The scene is flanked by palm trees, between which is a trilingual cuneiform inscription in Old Persian, Elamite and Babylonian, which reads 'I (am) Darius, great king.' (The word 'great' only occurs in Babylonian.) This was probably a seal of office.

Commentary on cat. nos 11–14

Stone seals with designs engraved in intaglio were in use in the Ancient Near East even before the invention of writing to indicate ownership and witness transactions. In the prehistoric period stamp seals predominate, but from about 3000 BC onwards the cylinder seal, usually engraved with an elaborate figural design, was the preferred form. These seals were rolled out on clay tablets inscribed in cuneiform as a form of signature. In the Late Assyrian and Neo-Babylonian periods in Mesopotamia (that is from about 800 BC down to 539 BC), however, stamp seals, now with beautifully engraved designs, became the most popular form. It is therefore surprising that in the Achaemenid period the cylinder seal makes something of a comeback, but this in itself may tell us something about Achaemenid art. The most famous Achaemenid cylinder seal is probably the Darius seal (cat. no. 14), which in some ways is deliberately archaizing. It shows the Persian king out in his chariot hunting lions rather in the manner of the Assyrian king Ashurbanipal, but here there are palm trees introducing Babylonia and a trilingual inscription in Old Persian, Elamite and Babylonian. This is, then, a wonderful example of the eclectic nature of Persian art, bringing different elements together and giving them a distinctive Persian appearance. This last element is indicated not just by the figure of the king, but also by the winged figure, Ahuramazda or the khvarnah, the god-given glory, hovering in the field above.

Other cylinder seals also hark back to traditional Ancient Near Eastern iconography, such as the chalcedony seal (cat. no. 13) which shows two heroic figures in combat with a lion and a bull respectively. One of the figures, that holding a lion, wears a Persian-style robe and a crown, and could represent the king himself, although this figure is usually referred to as 'the Persian royal hero'. However that may be, this is another example of taking an ancient motif and giving it a characteristically Persian appearance. The 'Persian royal hero' also features on stamp seals (for example, cat. no. 12) and stamp seal impressions where he is doing battle with a mythological creature such as a winged bull. This motif was also popular in monumental art at Persepolis, where it appears on stone reliefs in doorways. On our stamp seal the hero is wearing a typical Persian dress with folded pleats, giving the scene an unmistakable Persian identity. Another stamp seal (cat. no. 11) also bears a traditional scene, showing a rider on horseback hunting a wild goat; here the Achaemenid period identity of the seal is also established by the costume, but in this instance it is the Median dress of trouser suit and hood. In the Achaemenid period the semi-precious stone chalcedony was particularly popular for both cylinder seals and stamp seals.

In the present exhibition the glyptic art of the Achaemenid period is represented by four actual seals, but in fact it is better known through the large number of seal impressions on the Persepolis Fortification tablets and the Persepolis Treasury tablets, as well as on tablets found in Babylonia. There is also a large collection of cylinder and stamp seal impressions from Daskyleion in Turkey. It is interesting that variations of the royal archer motif that are found on coins from the royal mint (cat. nos 8–10) recur amongst the seal impressions from Persepolis.

As with some other art forms of this period, the seals demonstrate the re-use of traditional motifs but they are presented in a new way that is distinctively Persian.

Chapter V

The Oxus Treasure

The Oxus Treasure is a stunning collection of about 180 gold and silver objects that were originally found with a large number of coins probably on the north bank of the River Oxus at a site called Takht-i Kuwad in what is now Tajikistan, but was then in the Persian satrapy (province) of Bactria. Most of the objects date from the 5th–4th centuries BC, and it is thought they were probably donated to a temple over the course of several centuries. The Treasure includes some of the finest objects yet known from the Achaemenid period, and it is justly celebrated as one of the most splendid collections of goldwork from the ancient world.

One of the most outstanding pieces in the Treasure is a gold model chariot (fig. 67) with two wheels and pulled by four small horses. These may be early examples of a breed now known as Caspian horses, renowned for being small yet both sturdy and swift. In the chariot are two figures. The driver is standing and holds the reins in his hands. He wears a belted tunic and trousers and a hood with a pointed top. This outfit of trouser suit with a hood is generally known as the 'Median' costume. The passenger is seated on a bench that runs the length of the cab. He is also dressed in a 'Median' costume, but with an overcoat (*kandys*) slung over his shoulders. Both figures wear gold wire torques around their necks. On the front of the chariot car is a representation of the head of the Egyptian dwarf-god Bes, complete with feather crown. He was popular in the Persian empire, usually on amulets (fig. 79), and it is thought he had a protective function. The horses are hollow and made from pieces of gold sheet soldered together. Recent scientific analysis has shown that this chariot is almost certainly made of native alluvial gold containing silver to which copper was deliberately added. This chariot can be compared with the chariot shown on the Darius cylinder seal (cat. no. 14) and the king's chariots on the Apadana reliefs at Persepolis.

A second gold model chariot is now mostly incomplete, and although the driver is preserved the seated passenger is headless. A separate gold horse may have belonged with this chariot. Two sheet gold cut-out figures of horses were probably also parts of draught horses for a model chariot.

A solid gold rider figure wearing Median costume, with legs akimbo, may once have been mounted on a horse that is now missing. Two other small gold figures in Median costume (fig. 58) are now freestanding. Each wears a Median-style trouser suit with an overcoat (*kandys*) draped over the shoulders, leaving the sleeves empty. They wear a soft hood that covers the ears and chin. They each hold in their right hand a bundle of sticks (*barsom*). A larger statuette in silver, partially gilded, shows a bearded figure wearing a pleated robe in Persian style (fig. 59). On his

67 Gold model chariot pulled by four small horses from the Oxus Treasure. The two figures in the chariot are wearing Median trouser-suits, one with the addition of an overcoat (*kandys*). There is a head of Bes (see fig. 79) on the front of the chariot. 5th–4th century BC. British Museum (BM 123908, l. 18.8 cm).

head is a cap which is decorated with a band of incised crenellations around the top, which has led to suggestions that he might be a king. He is also carrying a bundle of sticks (*barsom*). Another large silver statuette is of a quite different type. This shows a youth with arms outstretched, completely naked except for a tall domed hat that is covered with gold foil. Hats of this kind are paralleled on the Persepolis reliefs and in Lydia, but nudity is unusual in the art of the Ancient Near East

68 (facing page) Gold scabbard for a short sword (*akinakes*) from the Oxus Treasure. The embossed and chased decoration on the scabbard shows the different stages of a lion hunt. 5th–4th century BC. British Museum (BM 123923, l. 27.6 cm). Drawing by Ann Searight.

and perhaps indicates Greek influence. This enigmatic figure is mounted on a square, stepped base. Again different is a large hollow gold head showing a beardless boy with short wavy hair and ears pierced for earrings. This was possibly part of a composite statue made of different materials including wood. The workmanship as well as the artistry is crude, and this head might have been locally produced.

Probably the most distinctive component of the Oxus Treasure is the fifty-one plaques made from thin sheet gold. They are mostly rectangular in shape, varying from just under 2 cm to almost 20 cm in height, and have chased (incised) designs, sometimes extremely crude, which usually show human figures (fig. 57). Some of the plaques were previously folded, but whether this happened in antiquity or in the 19th century is unknown. About thirty-seven of the human figures wear the so-called Median dress, sometimes with the addition of a long-sleeved overcoat (*kandys*) over the top of the belted tunic. In these cases the coat is shown draped over the shoulders with empty arms. Sometimes the Median dress is accompanied by a short Persian dagger (*akinakes*). The finest of these plaques is included in the exhibition (see cat. no. 7). In contrast to the popularity of the 'Median' costume, only about six of the figures on the plaques wear the so-called Persian dress consisting of a long robe with distinctive folds. One of the figures in Persian dress is possibly a woman. About twenty-five of the figures in Median dress are carrying the bundles of sticks or twigs known as *barsoms*. These are usually associated with Zoroastrian religious ceremonies and are generally carried by priests, although sometimes the *barsom* may simply have been a mark of devotion, as with the silver statuette of the king (see fig. 59).

Although none of the six figures in Persian dress is holding a *barsom*, at least four of them are holding a flower, as are seven of the figures in Median dress. The significance of this flower, which may be a lotus, is not clear, but at Persepolis it is sometimes held by the king himself. Lastly there are three plaques with animal representations that show respectively a horse, a donkey with large ears and a camel. Their inclusion in the Treasure is strange, as it is tempting to see the plaques as votive offerings made to a temple, and such plaques normally represent the supplicants, but possibly the animal plaques could also be votive, perhaps praying for the recovery of a sick animal or asking for the blessing of the deity. The great range of quality in these plaques is perhaps another indication that they were votive: some plaques seem to have been professionally executed, but others are so crude it looks as if they were scratched by the supplicants themselves. Non-destructive surface

analysis of thirty-eight of the fifty-one gold plaques in the Treasure suggest that alluvial god, alloyed with a little copper and possibly silver, was used for many of them. This alluvial gold could have been obtained from the upper reaches of the River Oxus where it is known to occur.

A gold scabbard cover for a Persian dagger (*akinakes*), one of the highlights of the Treasure (fig. 68), was partly mutilated, probably in the 19th century. The chape at the bottom of the scabbard is now missing. The thin gold, which was originally mounted on another material such as wood or leather, is embossed with scenes showing riders on horseback hunting lions, which are either shot with arrows or attacked with spears. In recent years, there has been much debate about the date of this scabbard cover. Because the hunting scenes are vaguely reminiscent of Assyrian reliefs from the time of Ashurbanipal (668–627 BC), and because the horsemen, although wearing trousers in the Iranian fashion, have fez-like hats similar to those worn by Assyrian kings, many scholars have seen this scabbard as one of the earliest pieces in the Oxus Treasure, perhaps even dating from the pre-Achaemenid Median period. However, other scholars have argued for a date not earlier than the time of Darius (522–486 BC), citing iconographic details such as the form of the winged disc above the pair of horsemen attacking a lion. A gold cut-out plaque in the shape of a bird's head (fig. 69) was probably fixed to the top of a bow-case (*gorytus*), as seen on the Persepolis reliefs.

69 (below) Gold cut-out plaque from theOxus Treasure in the shape of a bird's head with a large curved beak and a coiled serpentine neck. 5th–4th century BC. British Museum (BM 123940, h. 3.5 cm).

70 (facing page) Pair of gold bracelets from the Oxus Treasure with terminals in the form of monstrous animal heads. 5th–4th century BC. British Museum (BM 124047–8, diam. 7.9 cm).

Amongst the best-known objects in the Treasure is a pair of massive gold armlets with terminals in the form of horned, winged griffins (see cat. no. 17). In addition there are half-a-dozen spiral gold bracelets or torques with terminals in the form of lion's, ram's or goat's heads and eleven gold bracelets with abutting terminals in the form of winged goats and bull protomes, as well as the heads of lions, rams, goats, ducks and lion-griffins. Some of these bracelets have cavities for inlay, and in one case pieces of turquoise are still preserved. In a few cases the terminals have been cut off the original hoops, possibly soon after their discovery (see below), and remounted on modern silver or gold hoops. A particularly interesting pair of bracelets (fig. 70) has terminals in the form of monstrous animals with long snouts, triangular-shaped eyes and long tails which interlock at the back of the hoop. These bracelets seem to be related to the 'animal style' art of western Siberia that is often associated with the Scythians. There may also be Scythian influence in a heavy gold finger-ring (fig. 71) decorated in relief with the coiled figure of a lion. The twisting of animal bodies of animals into impossible circular shapes is a well-known characteristic of Scythian art. Another piece perhaps demonstrating Scythian influence is a splendid gold ornament in the form of a fabulous creature with the body of a winged goat and the head of a horned lion (fig. 72). This composite beast has its legs folded beneath it in the 'animal style' associated with the steppes of southern Russia. There are two long prongs at the back for attachment. It was most likely used as a hair or cap ornament. A gold roundel showing the head of a roaring lion, possibly further evidence of Scythian influence, was probably a horse harness decoration. Another item of harness (although it has sometimes been interpreted as a shield-boss) is a large silver gilt disc (fig. 73) with a circular composition showing horsemen hunting ibexes and deer. The style here is Achaemenid Persian.

The vessels in the Treasure include a gold bowl with embossed lions on the underside (see cat. no. 15), a shallow silver bowl that is also of

classic Achaemenid shape and has an embossed flower or rosette in the centre with fluted decoration in the form of radiating petals, and a gold jug with a lion's head at the top of the handle (fig. 74). Two further gold bowls in the Treasure are quite plain. A silver gilt figure of a leaping ibex is one of the two handles from a vase or amphora (fig. 75), probably of the same metal. Such vessels are shown on the reliefs at Persepolis being presented to the king by several of the delegations from different parts of the empire. A curious gold fish with a hollow centre and a hole in its mouth might also originally have been a vessel, but we do not know what sort of liquid it might have contained (see fig. 78).

Amongst other objects in the Treasure were more than a dozen circular gold plaques with various embossed designs including sphinxes, winged lions and a head of Bes (fig. 76). They were probably ornaments that could be sewn to or suspended from clothing. There were also twelve gold finger-rings, a chalcedony stamp seal and two cylinder seals. Three of the finger-rings and one of the cylinder seals show women, which is

71 (below left) Gold finger-ring from the Oxus Treasure with a large bezel decorated with in relief with a coiled figure of a lion. 5th–4th century BC. British Museum (BM 124012, diam. 2.5 cm)

72 (below right) Gold ornament from the Oxus Treasure representing on the front a recumbent lion-griffin. 5th–4th century BC. British Museum (BM 123924, l. 6.15 cm)

73 (bottom) Gilded silver and gold discs from the Oxus Treasure. The disc on the left shows riders on horseback hunting ibexes, and the disc on the right shows an eagle. They may both be horse harness ornaments. 5th–4th century BC. British Museum (BM 123925–6, diam. 9.65 and 9.8 cm).

74 Gold jug from the Oxus Treasure. 5th–4th century BC. British Museum (BM 123918, h. 13 cm).

unusual, as women are rarely depicted in the art of the Achaemenid period.

Originally about 1,500 coins were said to have belonged with the Treasure, but most of these cannot now be identified. There are, however, about 200 coins in the British Museum and more in other public collections such as the State Hermitage in St Petersburg which are thought by some scholars definitely to belong with the Treasure, but this is not accepted by all. However that may be, the coins include examples from mints around the Persian empire as well as from the reigns of Alexander and the Seleucid rulers who succeeded him in the eastern part of the Achaemenid empire. Sir Alexander Cunningham, who made a special study of the coins in the 19th century, concluded that they covered a period of about 300 years from the time of Darius to the reigns of Antiochus the Great (223–187 BC) and Euthydemus I of Bactria (*c*. 235–200 BC). If they were definitely part of the Treasure this would suggest that deposits were still being made until the late 3rd century BC, but the objects themselves appear to date from the 5th–4th centuries BC and material of obvious Hellenistic date is lacking. This is yet another of the unresolved enigmas surrounding the Oxus Treasure.

The Treasure was apparently found between 1876 and 1880 by local villagers on the banks of the River Oxus. They then sold it to three merchants from Bokhara, named Wazi ad-Din, Ghulam Muhammad and Shuker Ali, who regularly traded between Central Asia and India. They had with them a large amount of cash to buy tea, silk and other goods in India, and to avoid having to pay tax in Afghanistan they were anxious to convert their cash into commodities before crossing the Oxus. As they were making their way through Afghanistan, however, in May 1880, their caravan was held up by bandits between Kabul and Peshawar. The merchants' servant managed to escape, and he raised the alarm in the camp of a certain Captain Francis C. Burton. This Captain Burton had captained a Punjab battalion under Lord Roberts during the Second Afghan War (1878–80) and was now a political officer

75 Gilded silver handle in the form of a leaping ibex from a vase (amphora), from the Oxus Treasure. Vases of this kind are shown on the Persepolis reliefs. 5th–4th century BC. British Museum (BM 123911, h. 19 cm).

76 (facing page) Gold roundels from the Oxus Treasure which were probably dress ornaments or horse harness ornaments. 5th–4th century BC. British Museum (BM 123927–123936, 124065–124066, diamaters vary: 1.6–5 cm).

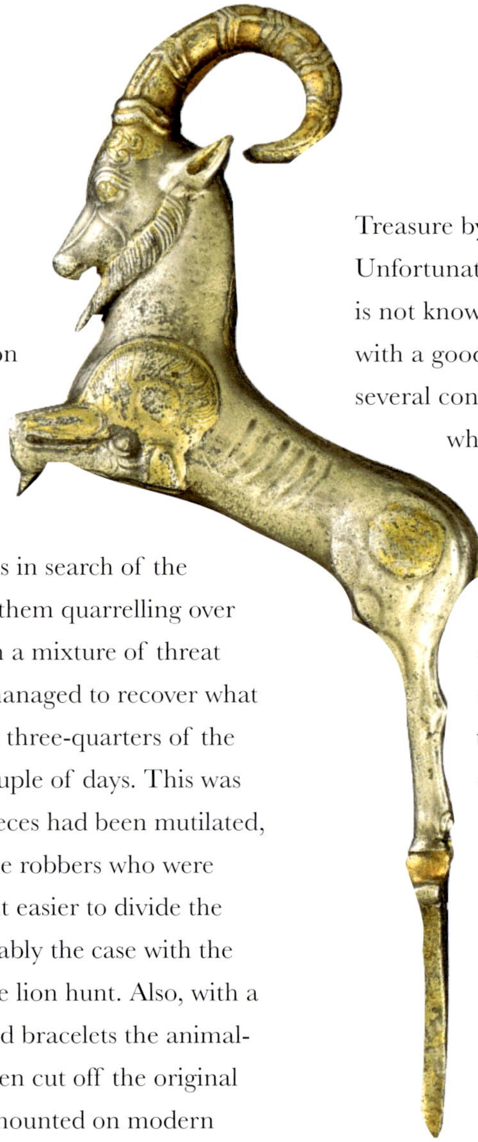

based at Seh Baba, three days' march from Kabul. His job was to keep open the lines of communication between Kabul and British India in the aftermath of the war. Burton immediately set out with a few orderlies in search of the bandits, and came across them quarrelling over their ill-gotten gains. With a mixture of threat and negotiation Burton managed to recover what is said to have been about three-quarters of the Treasure over the next couple of days. This was not before some of the pieces had been mutilated, however, apparently by the robbers who were cutting them up to make it easier to divide the spoils. This is most noticeably the case with the gold scabbard showing the lion hunt. Also, with a number of the torques and bracelets the animal-headed terminals have been cut off the original hoops and they are now mounted on modern hoops of silver, which is of course a less valuable material. Whether this mutilation occurred at this time or slightly later, however, it is impossible to say. After the Treasure had been returned to them the merchants continued on their journey to Peshawar.

This version of events comes mainly from the official British Museum catalogue of the Treasure by O.M. Dalton, first published in 1905. Unfortunately the source of Dalton's information is not known, and the story used to be viewed with a good deal of scepticism. Now, however, several contemporary reports have come to light which more or less corroborate Dalton's account. The most important of these is an account in the *Lahore Civil and Military Gazette* for 24 June 1880, which gives a detailed report of the incident including estimating the value of the gold at fifty to sixty thousand rupees and giving the extra detail that 180 men were involved in the hold-up. This incident is also recorded in Burton's official record of army service, where it is stated under 'Special Services in Peace or War' that Francis Charles Burton of the 2nd Bengal Lancers 'recovered the looted treasure taken from the *kafila* [i.e. caravan] of Central Asian and Samarkand merchants amounting to over Rs 60,000. Thanked by General Sir Donald Stewart'. What is not clear from either account is how many men Burton had at his disposal, but it was clearly more than 'the several orderlies' mentioned by Dalton.

Once the Treasure had been returned to them the merchants resumed their journey to Peshawar

and eventually sold the Treasure in Rawalpindi, both places in modern Pakistan. The pieces were then bought from dealers in the region either directly by General Sir Alexander Cunningham or through intermediaries by Sir Augustus Wollaston Franks (1826–97), Keeper of British and Medieval Antiquities at the British Museum, who was an avid and knowledgeable collector. Franks was later able to acquire the pieces owned by Cunningham, and when he died in 1897 Franks bequeathed to the British Museum his magnificent collections, including the Oxus Treasure.

The first publications of the coins and the gold and silver treasure by the numismatist Percy Gardner writing in the *Numismatic Chronicle* (1879, 1881) and by Sir Alexander Cunningham in the *Journal of the Asiatic Society of Bengal* (1881–3) all point to the site of Takht-i Kuwad on the north bank of the Oxus as being the likely find-spot. There are also Russian accounts to the same effect. In 1880 the Russian Major-General N.A. Mayev, who was in charge of an enquiry into the management of the Central Asian railway, described in a Russian newspaper article how gold objects found at Takht-i Kuwad had been sold to 'Indian' merchants. Then in 1889, a Russian officer, N.I. Pokotillo, wrote of Takht-i Kuwad: 'Despite the isolation of the site, there are always some tens of people there in search of treasure. They say someone once found a gold idol the height of a man.' Then, we have the slightly later testimonies of Russian scholars. In 1909, D.N. Logofet described Takht-i Kuwad as a site with ancient stone fortifications and referred to much gold having been found there and extensive illegal excavations. It also seems likely that A.A. Semenov was referring to the Oxus Treasure when he wrote in 1925: 'In 1917 the former Beg of Kobadian, Mirza Mahdibay, told me of remarkable finds [in ruins near Kobadian], in a mound half washed away by the waters of the river, consisting of metal objects which, judging from their description, were Achaemenid.'

The site of Takht-i Kuwad, named after the Sasanian king Kavad (i.e. 'throne of Kavad'), but written Kuwad in Russian, is a crossing point on the north bank of the River Oxus in modern Tajikistan. On the other side of the river is Afghanistan, and a ferry used to cross the river at this point. The site is now represented by a mound, on the top of which has been built a frontier post. There are apparently many signs of old excavations.

Takht-i Kuwad is about 5 km south of the citadel of the now famous site of Takht-i Sangin (fig. 77), where excavations have been in progress since 1976. A Soviet expedition led by B.A. Litvinsky and I.R. Pichikiyan worked at the site between 1976 and 1991, and since 1998 excavations have been directed by Angelina

77 Map showing where the Oxus Treasure was discovered.

Drujinina on behalf of the Tajik Academy of Sciences and the German Archaeological Institute. On the citadel is a monumental building which has been identified as a temple. The central columned hall of this temple was surrounded by storerooms containing more than 5,000 objects which had been dedicated to the temple. The collection included three gold votive plaques, one showing a man leading a camel, one showing a winged creature and one undecorated, portrait busts in clay and stucco, an ivory scabbard for a short sword (*akinakes*) carved with the figure of a lion, an elaborate ivory chape from a scabbard showing a fantastic creature who is part horse and part mermaid (*hippocamp*), an ivory lion protome from a rhyton as well as jewellery, weapons and coins.

Litvinsky and Pichikiyan believed that the Takht-i Sangin temple was built about 330–300 BC, as shown by the style of the Greek Ionic column capitals, and they dated the objects found inside it over a wide period from the 6th century BC through to the 2nd or 3rd century AD. Furthermore, they believed that some of the features they uncovered were fire altars and therefore identified the building as a fire temple, in which case it would have had connections with a form of the Zoroastrian religion. However, other scholars are doubtful about the interpretation as a fire temple and believe it is more likely the temple was dedicated to the god of the River Oxus. This is suggested by the discovery of a miniature altar dedicated to Silenus-Marsyas, the god of the Oxus.

The close proximity of Takht-i Sangin and Takht-i Kuwad raises intriguing questions about the relationship between the two sites and, indeed, the possibility that they were actually part of the same large complex in antiquity. There have even been suggestions that the Oxus Treasure originally came from Takht-i Sangin. This suggestion gains some credibility from the fact that the name of Takht-i Sangin is entirely modern, having been invented by Pichikiyan in the 1980s, and it is possible that in the 19th century the name of Takht-i Kuwad covered a wider area than it does now. However, the 19th-century accounts seem to be clear that the Oxus Treasure was found on the actual banks of the Oxus, which would appear to rule out the citadel at Takht-i Sangin, and in any case, while the dates of the two hoards overlap, there are some marked differences. Thus, while the Oxus Treasure seems to have been 'sealed' in the early 2nd century BC, the latest objects from Takht-i Sangin are 2nd or 3rd century AD. Secondly, while it is true that three gold 'votive' plaques have been found at Takht-i Sangin, neither in style, technique nor subject matter are they exactly the same as the Oxus Treasure plaques.

With the lack of reliable archaeological data, it is difficult to reach any definitive conclusions about the Oxus Treasure. However, the circumstantial evidence clearly indicates that the Oxus Treasure is a hoard, with the vast majority of the pieces dating from the 5th–4th centuries BC, and there is no reason to believe that any of the pieces are modern fakes, as has sometimes been claimed. What, then, could have been the purpose of this hoard? It is immediately striking that there are fifty-one gold plaques mostly with human representations that would seem to have been votive; that is, they were presented to a temple or a sanctuary to represent or bring favour to the donor. There are other figural representations in the Treasure that could have served the same purpose, such as the gold chariots with their passengers and the statuettes. It is possible, then, that the objects in the Treasure were presented to a temple over a long period of time, and indeed the non-figural objects in the Treasure, such as the jewellery and the gold and silver vessels, and also the coins, are typical of the type of precious objects that were presented to temples in the ancient world. If the objects in the Oxus Treasure were presented to a temple, what sort of temple was it? Admittedly we are here entering into the realms of speculation, but as this question is so important for the study of ancient Persian religion it cannot lightly be brushed aside. It cannot be a coincidence that no less than twenty-five of the gold plaques show figures dressed in the Median costume of trouser suit and hood and holding a *barsom*. These figures may have been priests, and they could have been involved in the worship of Ahuramazda. There may also be other elements of the Treasure that have religious connotations, such as the gold armlets with terminals in the form of griffins that could represent the Zoroastrian Veregna bird. The Veregna bird is associated with Verethragna, the victorious warrior god, and the kingly glory. More work on Zoroastrian imagery and iconography could well be informative for other objects in the Treasure. It seems possible then that the postulated temple had some connections with Zoroastrianism, or with a primitive form of Zoroastrianism that was centred on the worship of Ahuramazda.

Catalogue: Part 6

New Luxury Tableware

15

Oxus Treasure gold bowl

5th–4th century BC, Achaemenid period
Found on the north bank of the River Oxus (probably Takht-i Kuwad in present Tajikistan) between 1877 and 1880
Gold

H. 2.33 cm, Diam. 12.1 cm, Wt 73.5 g
BM 123919 (1897,1231.18)

This shallow gold bowl has a slight shoulder and a flared rim. There is a central boss (*omphalos*) hammered from the outside, and decoration to be seen from the underneath hammered from the inside. This embossed decoration on the underside shows two registers of almond-shaped lobes and between the larger lobes pairs of lions standing on their hind legs back to back and with their front legs arranged in a straight line behind and in front of their bodies.

78 Gold fish from the Oxus Treasure. It is hollow, and may have been used as a receptacle for liquids. 5th–4th century BC. British Museum (BM 123917, l. 24.2 cm).

16

Silver bowl with winged lions

5th–4th century BC, Achaemenid period
Find-spot unknown
Acquired 1971, offered 1970
Silver

H. 3.3 cm, Diam. 17.2 cm, Wt 300.9 g
BM 135571 (1971,0515.1)

This shallow silver bowl has a slight shoulder and a flared rim. There is a central boss (*omphalos*) on the inside and eight almond-shaped lobes on the underside. Between the lobes are applied silver cut-out figures of winged lions standing upright, each with the head and feather crown of the Egyptian dwarf-god Bes (fig. 79). There are small rosettes around the central boss and above each lion.

79 Faience pendant found at Persepolis showing the Egyptian dwarf-god Bes with a lion's face and a feather crown. Amulets and pendants showing Bes have been found all over the Persian Empire. In Egypt Bes protected women in childbirth, but outside Egypt he may have had a more general protective function. The winged lions on the silver bowl (cat. no. 16) have heads of Bes. 5th–4th century BC. National Museum of Iran (1206/7631, 7.3 x 3.8 cm).

Commentary on cat. nos 15–16

Shallow gold and silver bowls with an embossed centre (*omphalos*), slight shoulders (carinated) and flared rims are a characteristic feature of the Achaemenid period. They are sometimes referred to as phialai, but this is a term for Greek drinking bowls, not necessarily of this shape. The Achaemenid bowls sometimes have a lotus flower design. The shape of the bowls is derived from earlier Assyrian prototypes, but in the Achaemenid period the shoulders become less pronounced and the rims more flared. As a result, the Achaemenid bowls are quite distinctive and can be easily recognized. They also exist in bronze, glass and pottery. It is interesting that both of the above bowls were intended to be seen from underneath, when they were full of liquid and being held aloft on the tips of the fingers. Vessels like the Oxus Treasure gold bowl with embossed figures (cat. no. 15) are likely to have been the prototype for bowls with applied cut-out figures like the silver bowl (cat. no. 16). Applied figures of this kind, usually in gold, are found on a number of Achaemenid period vessels. The technique was probably first introduced in this period.

Gold and silver bowls were apparently common (fig. 80), particularly in privileged circles. According to Herodotus (*Histories* IX.80) the treasure found in the camp of the Persian general Mardonius after the Battle of Plataea in 479 BC included 'golden bowls and cups and other drinking-vessels'. Also, many drinking-cups of gold and silver were washed up ashore after the Persian fleet was wrecked off Magnesia (Herodotus VII.190). These bowls were presumably for drinking wine of which, according to Herodotus (I.133), the Persians were very fond. Unlike in Assyria, however, Achaemenid kings are never shown drinking from bowls of this kind.

80 (facing page) Achaemenid gold, silver and glass vessels in the British Museum collection. Lotus flower designs were very popular for shallow bowls. 5th–4th century BC.

Catalogue: Part 7

New Luxury Jewellery

17 Oxus Treasure gold armlet

5th–4th century BC, Achaemenid period
Found on the north bank of the River Oxus (probably Takht-i Kuwad in present Tajikistan) between 1877 and 1880
Gold

12.8 x 11.57 cm, Wt 397.1 g
BM 124017 (1897,1231.116)

This splendid gold armlet has terminals in the form of winged griffins. These monsters have the head and wings of a bird of prey, the body and forepaws of a lion and the horns and back legs of a goat. There are cells or *cloisons* for polychrome inlays on the heads, necks, wings and horns, and large cavities for inlays on the bodies of the animals. These inlays, which are now missing, would originally have been of coloured glass, faience and semi-precious stones such as turquoise, lapis lazuli and carnelian. The hoop of the armlet has a distinctive in-swing opposite the terminals. A companion armlet to this example was sold by Captain F.C. Burton to the Victoria and Albert Museum in 1884; it is now on long-term loan to the British Museum.

81 A tributary from delegation VI (Lydians) carrying armlets with griffin terminals similar to the Oxus Treasure examples, on the east side of the Apadana at Persepolis. Early 5th century BC.

Amongst the presents being brought for the king by the tribute delegations shown on the Apadana at Persepolis, bracelets were particularly popular, together with folded trouser suits and horses. Thus, large animal-headed bracelets are shown being presented to the king by four delegations, namely I (Medes), VI (Lydians) (fig. 81) and two Sythian tribes, XI (pointed-hat Scythians) and XVII (hauma-venerating Scythians). The bracelets being brought by the Lydian delegation have terminals in the form of winged griffins and are very similar to the Oxus Treasure examples. The popularity of the bracelets as diplomatic gifts accords with what Xenophon says in the *Anabasis* (1.2.27) when he records that Cyrus the Younger gave Syennis 'gifts which are regarded at court as tokens of honour – a horse with a gold-mounted bridle, a gold necklace and bracelets, a gold dagger and a Persian robe'.

There is a rich tradition of sumptuous jewellery in the Achaemenid period. We know this from representations of jewellery on the reliefs at Persepolis, on glazed brick panels from Susa and on statues in the round. There are also some magnificent surviving examples, in addition to those from the Oxus Treasure. Amongst these are a torque with lion's head terminals, bracelets, earrings and roundels, all with provision for

82 (left) Watercolor by Jacques de Morgan showing a burial discovered at Susa in 1901. The body, probably that of an elderly woman, was placed in a bronze coffin accompanied by a rich collection of jewellery. Musée du Louvre.

83 (below) A gold torque, gold bracelets and gold earrings found in the bronze coffin discovered at Susa in 1901. All of the pieces of jewellery have inlaid polychrome decoration. 5th–4th century BC. Musée du Louvre (Sb 2760–5).

84 (bottom) Pair of gold bracelets with ibex-head terminals from Pasargadae. These bracelets are decorated with fine wire ornamentation (filigree work) in spiral and plaited shapes. 5th–4th century BC. National Museum of Iran (3183, diam. 7.0 cm and 6.5 cm).

85 Pair of openwork gold earrings from Pasargadae decorated with granulation work (small gold balls). 5th–4th century BC. National Museum of Iran (3184, diam. 4.9 cm).

inlaid polychrome decoration, found in a tomb discovered by Jacques de Morgan in the Acropolis at Susa in 1901 (figs 82 and 83). Then there is a hoard of jewellery found in a pottery jar buried near one of the garden pavilions at Pasargadae, with ibex-headed gold bracelets (fig. 84) and openwork earrings (fig. 85). Achaemenid period jewellery found in tombs in Georgia and in the Lydian Treasure from western Turkey show that the tradition of fine jewellery extended all over the Persian empire. Some of the finest pieces of Achaemenid jewellery are characterized by their inlaid polychrome decoration, or at least provision for it, and such decoration is a hallmark of the Achaemenid period. In this tradition, pieces of jewellery were inlaid with semi-precious stones, coloured glass and paste. The inlays were held in place either by red-coloured cinnabar, which occurs naturally in Iran, or by bitumen. The inlays are fitted into cavities or cloisons on the surface of the goldwork, which has led to the term cloisonné decoration. This technique was not invented in the Achaemenid period – some earlier examples are attested – but it was brought by the Achaemenid goldsmiths to new levels of sophistication. Another remarkable achievement of this period is the great technical skill of the filigree and granulation work on some of the jewellery, particularly the pieces from Pasargadae.

Further Reading

The Many Meanings of the Cyrus Cylinder
'2600 years of history in one object', TED lecture by Neil MacGregor, 15 July 2011 (http://www.ted.com/talks/neil_macgregor_2600_years_of_history_in_one_object.html)

Chapter I: The Origins of the Persians
R. Bouckaert et al., 'Mapping the origins and expansion of the Indo-European language family', *Science*, 337 (2012), 957–60; V. Grugni *et al.*, 'Ancient migratory events in the Middle East: new clues from the Y-chromosome variation of modern Iranians', *PLoS ONE* (online journal) vol. 7, issue 7 (July 2012), pp. 1–14

Chapter II: History of the Persian Empire
Pierre Briant, *From Cyrus to Alexander: A History of the Persian Empire* (Winona Lake, Indiana, 2002)

Catalogue Part 1: A New Code of Ethical Behaviour
A. Kuhrt, 'The Cyrus Cylinder and Achaemenid imperial policy', *Journal for the Study of the Old Testament*, vol. 25 (1983), pp. 83–97; Mary Boyce, *Zoroastrians: Their Religious Beliefs and Practices* (London and New York 2001), pp. 50–3; E. Leichty, *The Royal Inscriptions of Esarhaddon, King of Assyria (680–669 BC), The Royal Inscriptions of the Neo-Assyrian Period Vol. 4* (Winona Lake, Indiana, 2011)

Cat. no. 1: The Cyrus Cylinder
I.L. Finkel (ed.), Proceedings of Cyrus Cylinder seminar, forthcoming; B.T. Arnold and P. Michalowski, 'Achaemenid period historical texts concerning Mesopotamia', in M.W. Chavalas (ed.), *The Ancient Near East* (Oxford 2006), pp. 426–30; C.B.F. Walker, 'A recently identified fragment of the Cyrus Cylinder', *Iran*, vol. 10 (1972), pp. 158–9; J.E. Curtis and N. Tallis, *Forgotten Empire: the World of Ancient Persia* (London 2005), no. 6; I.L. Finkel and M.J. Seymour (eds), *Babylon: Myth and Reality* (London 2008), pp. 78–9, 171–3; H. Rassam, *Asshur and the Land of Nimrod* (New York 1897); Shahrokh Razmjou, *The Cylinder of Cyrus the Great* (Tehran 2010) (in English and Persian); *The Cyrus Cylinder: National Museum of Iran*, exhibition catalogue (Tehran 2010) (in English and Persian)

Cat. no. 4: Brick with inscription of Cyrus
C.L. Woolley, *Ur Excavations IX: The Neo-Babylonian and Persian Periods* (London 1962), pp. 7–8; C.B.F. Walker, *Cuneiform Brick Inscriptions* (London 1981), no. 116; C.J. Gadd and L. Legrain, *Ur Excavation Texts*, vol. 1 (London 1928), no. 307

Chapter III: The Main Cities of the Persian Empire
D. Stronach, *Pasargadae* (Oxford 1978); Jean Parrot, *Le Palais de Darius à Suse* (Paris 2010); A.S. Shahbazi, *The Authoritative Guide to Persepolis* (Tehran 2004); P. Knapton, M.R. Sarraf and J.E Curtis, 'Inscribed column bases from Hamadan', *Iran* vol. 39 (2001), pp.99–117; I.L. Finkel and M.J. Seymour, *Babylon: Myth and Reality* (London 2008)

Catalogue Part 2: New Forms of Writing
Cat. no. 5: Fragment of column base with Old Persian inscription
P. Knapton, M.R. Sarraf and J.E. Curtis, 'Inscribed column bases from Hamadan', *Iran*, vol. 39 (2001), pp. 99–117; J.E. Curtis and N. Tallis, *Forgotten Empire: The World of Ancient Persia* (London 2005), no. 11; R.G. Kent, *Old Persian: Grammar, Texts, Lexicon* (2nd edn, New Haven, Connecticut 1953), no. A2Ha

Cat. no. 6: Pottery ostracon with Aramaic inscription
J. Naveh, 'The development of the Aramaic script', *Proceedings of the Israel Academy of Sciences and Humanities*, vol. 5 (1970), pp. 36–7; B. Porten and A. Yardeni, 'Three unpublished Aramaic ostraca', *Maarav*, vol. 7 (1991), pp. 207–27; J.E. Curtis and N. Tallis, *Forgotten Empire: The World of Ancient Persia* (London 2005), no. 312

Catalogue Part 3: A New Religion
P.R.S. Moorey, 'Religion and the rulers', *The Cambridge Ancient History: Plates to Volume IV* (Cambridge 1988), pp. 45–50; Mary Boyce, *Zoroastrians: Their Religious Beliefs and Practices* (London and New York 2001); Shahrokh Razmjou, 'Religion and burial customs', in J.E. Curtis and N. Tallis, *Forgotten Empire: The World of Ancient Persia* (London 2005), pp. 150–6; Elizabeth Errington

and Vesta Sarkhosh Curtis, *From Persepolis to the Punjab: Exploring Ancient Iran, Afghanistan and Pakistan* (London 2007), pp. 114–23; Wouter F.M. Henkelman, *The Other Gods Who Are: Studies in Elamite-Iranian Acculturation based on the Persepolis Fortification Texts*, Achaemenid History XIV (Leiden 2008)

Cat. no. 7: Oxus Treasure plaque with embossed and chased decoration showing a priest
O.M. Dalton, *The Treasure of the Oxus* (3rd edn, London 1964), no. 48; J.E. Curtis and N. Tallis, *Forgotten Empire: The World of Ancient Persia* (London 2005), no. 213; P. Amiet, 'Les ivoires achéménides de Suse', *Syria* 49 (1972), pl. V; K.A. Akishev, *Kurgan Issyk* (Moscow 1978) (in Russian)

Catalogue Part 4: A New Form of Currency
A.R. Meadows, 'The administration of the Achaemenid empire', in J.E. Curtis and N. Tallis, *Forgotten Empire: The World of Ancient Persia* (London 2005), pp. 181–209; Y. Lintz, 'The archer coins: a closer examination of Achaemenid art in Asia Minor', in J.E. Curtis and S.J. Simpson (eds), *The World of Achaemenid Persia* (London 2010), pp. 369–77

Cat. no. 8: Gold coin in form of a daric
J.E. Curtis and N. Tallis, *Forgotten Empire: The World of Ancient Persia* (London 2005), no. 321

Cat. no. 9: Silver coin in form of a siglos
J.E. Curtis and N. Tallis, *Forgotten Empire: The World of Ancient Persia* (London 2005), no. 320

Cat. no. 10: Silver coin in form of a stater
J.E. Curtis and N. Tallis, *Forgotten Empire: The World of Ancient Persia* (London 2005), no. 328

Catalogue Part 5: New Types of Seal
D. Collon, *First Impressions: Cylinder Seals in the Ancient Near East* (London 1987); P.H. Merrillees, *Catalogue of the Western Asiatic Seals in the British Museum, Cylinder Seals VI, Pre-Achaemenid and Achaemenid Periods* (London 2005); M.B. Garrison, 'Archers at Persepolis: the emergence of royal ideology at the heart of empire', in J.E. Curtis and S.J. Simpson (eds), *The World of Achaemenid Persia* (London 2010), pp. 337–59

Cat. no. 11: Stamp seal with hunting scene
J.E. Curtis and N. Tallis, *Forgotten Empire: The World of Ancient Persia* (London 2005), no. 422

Cat. no. 12: Stamp seal with hero fighting a winged bull
J.E. Curtis and N. Tallis, *Forgotten Empire: The World of Ancient Persia* (London 2005), no. 66

Cat. no. 13: Cylinder seal with figures fighting a lion and a bull
The Cambridge Ancient History: Plates to Volume IV (Cambridge 1988), no. 51b; P.H. Merrillees, *Catalogue of the Western Asiatic Seals in the British Museum, Cylinder Seals VI, Pre-Achaemenid and Achaemenid Periods* (London 2005), no. 30; J.E. Curtis and N. Tallis, *Forgotten Empire; The World of Ancient Persia* (London 2005), no. 72

Cat. no. 14: The Darius cylinder seal
P.H. Merrillees, *Catalogue of the Western Asiatic Seals in the British Museum, Cylinder Seals VI, Pre-Achaemenid and Achaemenid Periods* (London 2005), no.16; J.E. Curtis and N. Tallis, *Forgotten Empire; The World of Ancient Persia* (London 2005), no. 398; J.E. Curtis and N. Tallis, *The Horse: from Arabia to Royal Ascot* (London 2012), no. 107

Chapter V: The Oxus Treasure
O.M. Dalton, *The Treasure of the Oxus* (3rd edn, London 1964); J.E. Curtis, 'The Oxus Treasure in the British Museum', *Ancient Civilizations from Scythia to Siberia*, vol. 10 (2004), pp. 294–338; J.E. Curtis, *The Oxus Treasure: British Museum Objects in Focus* (London 2012)

Catalogue Part 6: New Luxury Tableware
P.R.S. Moorey, 'The technique of gold-figure decoration on Achaemenid silver vessels and its antecedents', *Iranica Antiqua*, vol. 23 (1988), pp. 231–51; S.J. Simpson, 'The royal table', in J.E. Curtis and N. Tallis, *Forgotten Empire: The World of Ancient Persia* (London 2005), pp. 104–11

Cat. no. 15: Oxus Treasure gold bowl
O.M. Dalton, *The Treasure of the Oxus* (3rd edn, London 1964), no. 18; J.E. Curtis and N. Tallis, *Forgotten Empire: The World of Ancient Persia* (London 2005), no. 100

Cat. no. 16: Silver bowl with winged lions
J.E. Curtis and N. Tallis, *Forgotten Empire: The World of Ancient Persia* (London 2005), no. 101

Catalogue Part 7: New Luxury Jewellery
I. Özgen and J.Öztürk, *Heritage Recovered: the Lydian Treasure* (Istanbul 1996); P.R.S. Moorey, 'Material aspects of Achaemenid polychrome decoration and jewellery', *Iranica Antiqua*, vol. 33 (1998), pp. 155–71; J.E. Curtis, 'Jewellery and personal ornaments' in J.E. Curtis and N. Tallis, *Forgotten Empire: The World of Ancient Persia* (London 2005), pp. 132–49; J.Y. Chi (ed.), *Wine, Worship and Sacrifice: the Golden Graves of Ancient Vani* (New York 2008)

Cat. no. 17: Oxus Treasure gold armlet
O.M. Dalton, *The Treasure of the Oxus* (3rd edn, London 1964), no. 116; J.E. Curtis and N. Tallis, *Forgotten Empire: The World of Ancient Persia* (London 2005), no. 153

Picture Credits

(All numbers refer to fig. numbers unless otherwise specified)

© The National Gallery, London 2013: p. 9

British Museum (© Trustees of the British Museum): p. 11, p. 13, Cat. nos. 1–17, 7, 10, 13, 15, 28, 30, 33, 43, 45, 48, 47, 57–9, 61, 63–4, 67–76, 78, 80

Courtesy of the Thomas Jefferson Collection of the Rare Book Division of the Library of Congress: p. 12

©AFP/Getty Images: p. 15 (left), 17, 18

Photograph © John Curtis: 1, 3, 6, 9, 14, 16, 20–1, 23–4, 27, 34, 35, 37, 38, 39–42, 49–55, 61–2, 65–6, 81

Map by Martin Brown: 2, 8, 77

© National Museum of Iran, all photography by Ebrahem Khadem-Bayat: 4, 32, 44, 46, 60, 79, 84–5

Ministry of Defence: 19

© The British Library Board: 22 (Add. MS 14758(i) 46/56)

© Photo RMN: 29 (Franck Raux), 31 (Hervé Lewandowski), 82, 83 (Lee Oi-Cheong)